Praise for *Off the Tracks*

"I read *Off the Tracks* in one sitting, on a couch by a window that transformed into a European couchette, a stagecoach, a dining car speeding through a Maritime landscape and more on journeys that were remembered, imagined, and hoped for. Sparked by a stillness in time, Mulloy writes in beautiful, spare prose of travel as an act of the mind and memory, the ever-changing notion of home, and covers landscapes that are both geographic and metaphoric. Her travelling companions are historic as well as intimate, and always interesting, while Mulloy is a thoughtful, nuanced, and engaging guide." —EMILY URQUHART, author of *Ordinary Wonder Tales*

"Pamela Mulloy's *Off the Tracks* is like 'slow travel' itself: absorbing, with many grace notes of observant and profound perceptions on the whole  preferably by train. Like storyteller, allowing her open doors onto travel's re itics, and the whole project of selfhood. Perceptively written, it is full of fascinating insights on how travel allows us to discover and understand our world." —JEAN MCNEIL

"Mulloy sends us vivid dispatches on the beautiful topic of trains and train dreams, leaping easily from the Napoleonic Wars to Google Maps, botany and Brontë to Italian movies. *Off the Tracks* recounts both psychic and physical journeys, past and present, parallel trips to international destinations, and, perhaps more importantly, the in-between places of travel. This is an intimate memoir, brimming with pleasing tangents and informed by family, history, lit, and wit." —MARK ANTHONY JARMAN, author of *Touch Anywhere to Begin*

PAMELA MULLOY

Off *the* Tracks

A MEDITATION ON TRAIN JOURNEYS IN A TIME OF NO TRAVEL

ECW

Published by ECW Press
665 Gerrard Street East
Toronto, Ontario, Canada M4M 1Y2
416-694-3348 / info@ecwpress.com

Editor for the Press: Susan Renouf
Copy editor: Jen Knoch
Cover design: Caroline Suzuki
Front cover photograph © David Lichtneker /
Arcangel Images

LIBRARY AND ARCHIVES CANADA CATALOGUING
IN PUBLICATION

Title: Off the tracks : a meditation on train
journeys in a time of no travel / Pamela Mulloy.

Names: Mulloy, Pamela, 1961- author.

Identifiers: Canadiana (print) 20230567800 |
Canadiana (ebook) 2023056786X

ISBN 978-1-77041-729-8 (softcover)
ISBN 978-1-77852-255-0 (ePub)
ISBN 978-1-77852-256-7 (PDF)

Subjects: LCSH: Railroad travel—History.

Classification: LCC G156 .M85 2024 | DDC
910.4—dc23

This book is funded in part by the Government of Canada. *Ce livre est financé en partie par le gouvernement du Canada.* We acknowledge the support of the Canada Council for the Arts. *Nous remercions le Conseil des arts du Canada de son soutien.* We acknowledge the funding support of the Ontario Arts Council (OAC), an agency of the Government of Ontario. We also acknowledge the support of the Government of Ontario through the Ontario Book Publishing Tax Credit, and through Ontario Creates.

ONTARIO ARTS COUNCIL
CONSEIL DES ARTS DE L'ONTARIO
an Ontario government agency
un organisme du gouvernement de l'Ontario

Canada Council   Conseil des arts
for the Arts   du Canada

Canadä

PRINTED AND BOUND IN CANADA   PRINTING: MARQUIS   5   4   3   2   1

MIX
Paper from
responsible sources
FSC® C103567

For
Darren
and for
Esme

Travel is the most private of pleasures. There is no greater bore than the travel bore.

—Vita Sackville-West, *Passenger to Teheran*

I'm not much of a traveller at all. I travel in order to keep still. I want to be in or move through empty spaces in circumstances where nothing much will happen.

—Jenny Diski, *Stranger on a Train: Daydreaming and Smoking Around America with Interruptions*

But travel must be an extravagance, a sacrifice to the rules of chance, from daily life to the extraordinary; it must represent the most intimate and original form of our taste.

—Stefan Zweig, *Journeys*

Contents

The Primacy *of* Slowness

1

The Year *of* No Travel

22

Uncoupling

34

The Tedium *of* Velocity

43

The Grand Tour

62

Escape: *The* Train Compartment

76

Women *and* Travel

88

Tycoons *and* Explorers

106

Pathologies: Train Accidents *and* Illnesses

121

The Train Station

134

The Extraordinary Ordinary: Ways *to* Travel

147

Borders

159

Afterword

167

Selected Bibliography

175

Acknowledgements

177

The Primacy *of* Slowness

Trains were a novelty to Ernestine; they were fascinating, unknown, terrible. What were they like as they came tearing their way through the valley, plunging between the mountains as if not even the mountains could stop them? When she saw the dark, flat breast of the engine, so bare, so powerful, hurled as it were towards her, she felt a weakness; she could have sunk to the earth. And yet she must look.

—Katherine Mansfield, "Father and the Girls"

From my window I see an angel in the garden of my neighbour. This angel is about the size of an eight-year-old child and is alabaster white. It is turned away from me, and I see a gentle wave of hair that falls to the shoulders, a set of wings that shroud the body like the hunched ones of an eagle. The feathers sculpted on the wings like tufted meringue. The angel is turned away from me now, but when it first appeared, I'm sure it was facing me. I try not to read anything into this.

1

I can't remember if the angel appeared before or after the pandemic started, and again I try not to read anything into its sudden appearance. I first saw the angel across the street when another neighbour was walking it out to the edge of the road with a sign that said "FREE" hanging around its neck. The neighbours who claimed it are not religious people as far as I know. More likely to pray to the goddess of seventies rock music since they play in a band, as evidenced by the steady drum beat on Thursday nights that comes from their basement. They are pleased with the legalization of pot.

My view of the angel was a constant in those first pandemic weeks, a welcome focus when I swivelled my chair to look out the window, where before I saw only the brick house, the back deck occasionally peopled with my next-door neighbours and their friends. Time slowed, spring burst forth, then retreated, the angel momentarily lost in a whirl of snow. And people talked of calm, of a peacefulness that descended like that persistent snow. Some talked of boredom, but at this moment we had not yet been stricken. The stillness constant, our house a ship becalmed.

For the past twelve years, on a day late in June I have boarded a train in Kitchener, Ontario, with my daughter, Esme, the first time when she was just five years old. Two further trains and twenty-seven hours later we disembark in Moncton. In those first moments as we roll out of town, we point out rat boxes behind the bread factory, fishermen on the shores of the Grand River, and, gaining speed, we poise ourselves at the window to catch a glimpse of what we've dubbed "the castle house," a garish paradox amid this pastoral farmland, with its battlement roof and gated boundary. Who are they trying to keep out, I wonder. From our window, we have the perfect, albeit fleeting, view of the castle house and it feels like our secret discovery, an intrusion on those owners who want to be seen and not seen.

This seeing and not seeing is what we do during this entire journey: a rusted car, a stack of firewood, an empty swimming pool. Our eyes drift to the outer landscape, to the panoramic view, then flicker back to what is immediately before us, rushing by.

This back and forth, this shifting perspective is something we take for granted, so accustomed we are to this mode of travel we now consider "slow." We are given a view, framed by the window, and have time to take it in, our eyes scanning lazily as though hypnotizing ourselves into a meditative state.

If we were a mother and daughter travelling in the nineteenth century, before trains came into popular use, we might travel by stagecoach and in so doing have an even more intimate connection to the flowers and trees outside our window. We would feel the breeze, perhaps tug at a shawl against the chill, hear voices of travellers on the road, or of farmers in passing fields. This is a connection we rarely have now with our environment as we travel. Our aim is to move swiftly, to get to our destination as quickly as possible. Who has time to determine what sort of hawk that is flying overhead?

If we were travelling when trains came into use, we might have been agitated by the speed of this new technology, which had so many images storming past our window. We would not be able to smell the lilacs, acknowledge the faces of those standing on the roadside or in a field, see the detail in the flowers on the embankment. Victor Hugo described the view from a train in a letter dated 22 August 1837: "The flowers by the side of the road are no longer flowers but flecks, or rather streaks, of red and white . . . the grain fields are great shocks of yellow hair; field of alfalfa, long green tresses; the towns, the steeples, and the trees perform a crazy mingling dance on the horizon; from time to time, a shape, a spectre appears and disappears with lightning speed behind the windows; it's a railway guard."

In the time of pandemic slowness, when we were considering the condition of the entire planet, when we couldn't travel anywhere, I decided to go back in time, to think of the social history of train journeys, not only in longing, but also to understand what it is that we gain in movement, in travel. In doing this I wanted to think about what we see, and how we observe, on such journeys. I was thinking of that imagined stagecoach journey, and the actual train trips I've taken, and those I hope to take. There are also fictional and remembered conversations with fellow travellers over the years, those casual, intimate, sometimes intense exchanges that can come through travel, when something in us has loosened. All that was beyond us as we sat in our homes, and so this remembering and reflecting felt all the more urgent.

On our annual journey, the train is often running late, and as it moves through the dry Ontario countryside, I begin to worry about the connection to Montreal at Union Station in Toronto. My eyes settle on the parched Ontario farmland and I am reminded of my own childhood summers on my grandparents' farm in Prince Edward Island: the dry heat, the dust in the yard, the scratch of hay against my bare legs as I hoisted bales onto the trailer. My daughter's summers are marked by travel—to one set of grandparents in the Maritimes, then later to the other set in England. When we journey this way, our backpacks are filled with books, notebook and pens, a computer for movie watching later on. Our trip begins with the stillness that allows us to indulge in these pursuits. In this age of air travel, it is but a slow swagger across the landscape. We can read, write, think, or daydream. Later we will succumb to the screen.

Coming into Toronto, there is an abrupt loss of green, the savagery and banality of this entrance into the city—a mountain of broken pallets, gas canisters lined up like soldiers, rows of truck containers, loading docks, roads criss-crossing, a patch of wild grass, electrical pylons like giants passing rope to each other. The entrance to a city by train is rarely marked by beauty. Instead, there is a messiness to it that feels true and authentic of what's really going on, the functions laid bare. Like the tangle of shoes at the back door that says, yes, we live here.

A quick change of train at Union Station with my daughter in charge of counting bags—an annual responsibility first assigned when she was five—while I hold the tickets and determine our car number. We find our seats, claim what we need from our bags for this five-hour leg. Time feels fluid and restlessness sets in as I flitter from writing to reading, and for her, a video game or listening to music while reading. At times we stare out the window in a dreamy state, the view ordinary and familiar. We don't fully settle in, for the coach is full and noisier than we want it to be and we are anticipating the next train we'll board in Montreal, the one where we will be in a cabin.

That train is called the Ocean, the longest-running named train in Canada. In 2003 it celebrated its centenary, and in the hundred plus years it's been operating, it has had the same route: Montreal to Halifax. On this train, we often see the poet Zach Wells, whom I know from my work. He works on the Ocean as a service manager, and it has been our ritual to seek him out. When he is not working on our train, we are disappointed. Once, when we were sitting in the dining car, he stopped to chat and in the midst of our conversation we heard the voice of the engineer on Zach's radio announce that there was a moose on the right side of the train, and he pointed it out as we flew by it. It is this moose I think about when I remember Victor Hugo's sentiment—catching a glimpse that becomes a blur we barely register.

※

"What is it," a friend asked, "that draws you to trains?" A question for which the answer seemed both obvious and ungraspable. In this time of the pandemic there will be no train journeys so I am left to consider this question. Yes, indeed, why trains? I have no ready answer for my friend and so when I can't explore the question by travelling again, I decide that I will explore it through past experiences, lost opportunities.

Why trains? I expect it is, for me, to be moving, to be going somewhere. And I anticipate that this act of remembering and imagining trains and travel will find it to be true. The anticipation of travel, as well as the looking back, tends to take me partway into the journey. I enter this psychic space and feel both the calm and thrill of actual travel. This compulsive imagining is mind-travelling, a kind of simulation of the actual journey. Fanciful but effective nonetheless.

In Montreal we enter our cabin, a bench on one side that will turn into two bunks, space under it for our suitcases, a narrow cupboard where we can hang any garments if we had any that needed hanging, and a bathroom where you can brush your teeth while you sit on the loo if you are so inclined. In a wall pocket by the window there is a booklet with historical or cultural tidbits about each of the twenty-eight stops on our route. Number 9, Trois-Pistoles, Quebec, Mile 161.7: "Legend has it that a French sailor passing through the region in the 17th century lost his silver goblet, worth three gold pistols (an old type of coin) in the nearby river. That's how a very picturesque name was given to the river and later to this small industrial town on the Lower St. Lawrence." Number 27, mile 0.4: "Truro is home to the famous Stanfield Underwear Company, which invented cotton stretch knitwear and the trap door in long johns . . ."

Soon after the train leaves Montreal on the last trip we took before the pandemic we are called to dinner for the first sitting. We make our way to the dining car, tickets in hand, and are seated, a table for four with a white linen tablecloth and napkins. We are joined by a woman in her late sixties, a professor of anthropology, and then Heather, an administrator at a hospital (overqualified, she assured us) sits down, wide-eyed and chatty. She tells us about clearing out her father's basement after he died and finding live bullets from World War II. Then she talks about the Halifax Riots on VE-Day, when soldiers and sailors waiting to depart for Europe rioted after the fearful city declared a no-liquor policy.

The anthropologist, whose name we never find out, tells us that she makes this journey twice a year, from Vancouver to Halifax. She is terrified of flying. She once made a trip from Washington State to China by land and sea—two ships and several trains. On one trip the return sea voyage was cancelled and she was stranded in Beijing. She called her sister-in-law in Newfoundland who agreed to fly all the way to Beijing to accompany her onto a plane. They spent a week together in the city, then with the help of five Ativan she boarded the plane and slept most of the way. Once, when she did wake, she told her sister-in-law that she would need a wheelchair to get off the plane. We talk to these women about my daughter's interest in social history and her passion for Ruth Goodman's living history documentaries on the BBC.

For that hour we are dinner companions, revealing more of ourselves than intended. We eat our dinner, drink our wine, while outside the Quebec landscape is turned a crimson orange by the setting sun.

On these journeys we are often taken to a table of four and joined by two strangers. The forced intimacy differs from the sense of separateness we feel on the rest of the trip. I liken it to stagecoach journeys, where conversation was said to be natural and expected.

The stagecoach encouraged rapport because the passengers were snugly packed inside and out—with some sitting on top or next to the coachman. This gave everyone a sense of shared experience, travellers, coachman, and guard alike. A passenger might call out to the driver to check on the weather, or make an observation on passing crops, or ask a question about accommodations. There would surely be the feeling of having more control over the journey than we do now in a train or plane. Could we ask to stop if we felt sick, if we wanted to take a closer look at the brook we've just crossed? For stagecoach travellers there was a more immediate connection to each other and to the passing landscape.

For passengers on the first trains in Europe, which were designed with isolated compartments without a corridor, the train guards and porters were physically separated from them during the trip, so there was no opportunity to point out landmarks or respond to questions about arrival times. In addition, the train itself was too loud and too fast to be conducive to much banter, and most conversations were limited to initial niceties and requests to open or close the window. This soon brought about a social shift that was frequently written about in publications such as *The Railway Traveller's Handy Book*: "Generally speaking, the occupants of a railway carriage perform the whole of the journey in silence; but if one passenger be more loquaciously inclined than the rest, he is soon silenced by abrupt or tart replies . . ." Of her journey in a railway compartment, the American writer Harriet Beecher Stowe observed that "a stranger might travel all through England, from one end to the other and not be on conversing terms with a person in it."

This was in first class. In third class the mood was altogether more raucous as noted by French novelist Alphonse Daudet: "I'll never forget my trip to Paris in a third-class carriage . . . in the midst of drunken sailors singing, big fat peasants sleeping with their mouths open like those of dead fish, little old ladies with their baskets, children, fleas, wet nurses, the whole paraphernalia of the carriage of the poor with the odour of pipe smoke, brandy, garlic sausage and wet straw. I think I'm still there."

In North America the carriages were designed with an open interior, benches on both sides and a coal stove in the middle.

Charles Dickens describes them as being "like shabby omnibuses, but larger" and was struck by the freedom of speech that prevailed where the conversation could range from politics to banking to the price of cotton. "Everybody talks to you, or to anybody else who hits his fancy."

Train travel today carries some of both these attitudes. Once in my twenties when travelling the Ocean on my own, I entered the packed dining car and, along with the man before me in the queue, was shown to a table where two men were sitting, an MP who was on his way home to New Brunswick and a truck driver going on holiday. The young man who had joined the table with me, who the others thought was my partner and whose face was painted blue, had come directly to the train after the Bastille Day celebrations. The MP kept the conversation moving along as best as one could with such disparate company, especially when one of the passengers is a blue-faced man, and it turned out to be a jolly evening with conversation zig-zagging across various points of interest.

We have become accustomed to the imposed company that comes with travel, the mixing of strangers, the confined space, yet the ability to go to the dining car and engage in such a fundamental ritual as eating together creates a small society. Sometimes we are in solitude in this society, sometimes we make connections.

At night, back in our cabin, my daughter and I feel indulged, this privacy so complete. We hear footsteps walking down the corridor but know they have nothing to do with us. It is as though we are secret travellers, hidden in our little room. We jostle for seating, negotiating over what we want to see. Esme looks ahead to what is coming our way, her eyes adjusting to the momentary images flashing by while I, with my back to the wall, legs stretching towards the window, look straight out. Mine is not so much a view but a smear of colours and shapes. We are still part of this outside world, but only tangentially, and soon when darkness falls, we will close the curtains and the sense that it is just the two of us will be complete. We are longing to get into our bunks, but we don't want to rush the evening. The steady clacking of the rails like a metronome gives a counter beat to our own internal rhythm.

It is at some point around this time that we truly slip into another version of ourselves. One that is separated from work or school, from routine and deadlines. One that can settle into another way of being, where time actually slows, allowing something that is not exactly boredom but a version of it, one that makes us feel calm and free. This is what I missed in our time of no travel. Time slowed, yes, but it was more treacle-like as I soldiered on with work, and the boredom was dull and flat even as I tried to fold in some activity—a day at the beach, a walk with a friend—that might feel like a short holiday. The shift I feel on trains seems to happen on a cellular level, where my whole body gives into it, my mind sighing with relief.

When we finally succumb to our beds, having summoned the attendant to pull down the top bunk and get the bedding out, I feel cradled, not as recalled memory from childhood, but as a comfort that feels necessary and normal. The bunk is narrow—I have to shimmy across and lift myself when turning over—but it is room enough. I settle into my pillow, position my book with a booklight attached, and pull the duvet over me. My daughter clambers up the ladder to her bunk and is doing much the same. Now we two are separate, each in our night cave, the train rocking us, gently, until we hit a bump that bounces us, and we laugh as if we are on a fairground ride. But mostly it's a soothing sway, and soon we are tired and can no longer read. When the lights are out, we are still moving with the train, our limbs loosened, our muscles relaxed, our minds slowly drifting off.

In the days before the Ocean ran along this line, the trains were run by the Intercolonial Railway (ICR), their tracks laid down as far away as possible from the United States border; the War of 1812 had left officials wary of cross-border invasion. With no standard track sizes yet, the Province of Canada adopted a five-foot six-inch gauge in 1851 that differed from those built in American states, further preventing any rail movement between the two countries. One of the early cars on the ICR route was built by Pullman Palace Car Company. Under the agreement, Pullman agreed to provide the cars and porters and maintain the linen, upholstery, and carpets. One of the first cars to arrive, called the Moncton, was described by a reporter as the "best car ever . . . the inside finish is all done with imported woods and it is very tasty."

The Ocean Limited was launched in July 1904, and included the sleeping car Quebec, a first-class coach, a baggage car, and a colonist car. The Quebec was put on display before departure and was described by a reporter as having "highly polished walnut in the wood which has been used for the interior, combined with the green plush upholstering of the seats and the green carpet, gives the cars an appearance of great luxury and comfort."

These luxury cars were a sharp contrast to the colonist cars purchased to handle the European immigrant influx that boomed as the Canadian Pacific Railway (CPR) was expanding in the northwest. Introduced in the 1880s, the colonist cars ran until the 1960s and replaced the earlier crude immigrant cars that were essentially grain boxcars with benches. The colonist cars had wooden slat seats and folding upper berths that were accessed by the one ladder in the car. While the passengers had these accommodations where they could lie down, they had to provide their own mattress and bedding and had to remain dressed as there were no berth curtains.

Around the time of World War I, a family could cross Canada for seven dollars. Immigrants arriving at the eastern seaports were put on the trains headed to various locations. Robbie Waisman, a Jewish war orphan and Holocaust survivor who arrived in 1948, had hoped to go to either Montreal to use his French or Toronto where he had connections, but against all common sense was put instead on a train to Calgary.

❧

There are other, less mentioned stories that are part of this one of expansion—one of which is the impact on Indigenous people already living on the land where tracks were to be laid and colonizers settled. The government saw the trains as necessary to move lumber, coal, stone and other materials required to build a settler nation, as well as to move the people who would occupy these lands. The plan was conceived with little or no regard to those who were native to this territory. It was as if they weren't there, other than as an obstacle to be moved out of the way.

In 2020, modern settlers were forced to consider the tainted history of the railway companies that had gotten rich on land once inhabited by Indigenous peoples when supply chains and commuter routes were disrupted. In protest to the Coastal GasLink Pipeline that was scheduled to run though Wet'suwet'en territory in British Columbia, Indigenous groups and supporters across the country set up blockades on commuter railways that not only highlighted this current invasion, but also reminded us that the country was built by displacing Indigenous people from their homes, often moved to less arable land, or away from waterways from which they fed their families. "I never ever thought that we as Wet'suwet'en people would ever be faced with such a crisis we're facing today," Hereditary Chief Kaliset told CBC news.

In 1880, five thousand Indigenous people were removed from Cypress Hills, Saskatchewan, to make way for the Canadian Pacific Railway. This is just one example of the coercive relocation that took place. With diminishing bison herds leaving many Indigenous communities without a major food source, the federal government used the promise of food to move thousands of people away from the rail line. This food supply was limited, and many starved. According to James Daschuk, who wrote about the "subjugation and forced removal of indigenous communities from their traditional territories" in his book *Clearing the Plains*, "Once on reserves, food placed in ration houses was withheld for so long that much of it rotted while the people it was intended to feed fell into a decades-long cycle of malnutrition, suppressed immunity and sicknesses from tuberculosis and other diseases. Thousands died."

The impact of the railway went beyond loss of land and livelihood for Indigenous peoples. Those very emigrants who travelled across the country in their colonist cars to settle this newly occupied land also brought with them diseases, such as measles and influenza, that would devastate the Indigenous peoples already living there.

During a number of recent protests, those protesting were able to reclaim some of the power their forebears had lost. As many whose ancestors had lost their homes when the railway came roaring through, the fact that they had the power to halt the trains and reclaim this space had emotional significance. They held up trains that transported people and grain as way of saying, I'm here, I've always been here. In referring to the protests, Unist'ot'en Hereditary Spokesperson Freda Huson stated: "Our people's belief is that we are part of the land. The land is not separate from us. The land sustains us. And if we don't take care of her, she won't be able to sustain us, and we as a generation of people will die."

Another largely hidden expansion story is the contribution that Chinese workers made in extending the transnational railway to British Columbia. It's estimated that 17,000 Chinese workers came to Canada to complete the construction, which took four years. They were paid one dollar a day from which they had to pay for their provisions, as compared to white workers who were paid between $1.50 to $2.50 and didn't have to pay for their provisions. Some 700 died as a result of unsafe conditions during the construction. Despite their significant contribution to the building of the railway, they are notably absent from the famous photograph in which CPR Director Donald Alexander Smith drove the "last spike" that connected the east and west legs of the railway. In 1989, their work was finally publicly recognized when a memorial erected in Toronto was dedicated to their contribution.

～✿～

In the morning when we awake in our bunks, we look out along Chaleur Bay in northern New Brunswick, to this body of water that reaches out to the ocean. A scenic route, this stretch, a break from the interminable trees. I lie in my bunk and look out at the steel grey sky, at the cottages that dot the beachfront and wonder how it is that I, who so longs for the sea, now live in a landlocked region.

It is a balm, this view of endless water, and I'm reminded of a train in Brighton, England, I once read about known as the Daddy Long Legs, for it ran along the sea. On November 28, 1896, Magnus Volk, an entrepreneur who was the first to install electric light in his home, saw his spectacular vision of a seaside railway connecting Brighton to Rottingdean, a village three miles to the east, come to fruition. The train was launched with the mayor and mayoress of Brighton on board and featuring a ceremonial lunch, and was by all accounts a successful journey. What made this train, officially called the Pioneer, unique was that it was suspended above the sea, supported by twenty-three-foot-high struts with an eighteen-foot-wide base that allowed the train to run over the water along the beach between the two towns. Due to regulations, a sea captain was required on board at all times, and life jackets were given to the travellers.

A week after the Daddy Long Legs was launched, a storm blew in, damaging electric wires and part of the track. Undaunted, Volk immediately set to repairing the railway, including the Pioneer itself that had been knocked on its side, and it was relaunched the following July.

That would have been a sublime journey, I think, the sensation of flying—for this was a term often used to describe train travel at the time—of being on the sea but not entirely in it. Would it feel as if you were soaring with seagulls?

It is a trip I would have loved to take. The railway no longer exists, but for the short time of its operation it spoke to the wildly imaginative innovation that was characteristic of the end of the nineteenth century. The Exposition Universelle of 1900 in Paris introduced subways, moving sidewalks, talking films, escalators, a Ferris wheel, matryoshkas—known more commonly as Russian nesting dolls—and the spectacular display of an electricity fairy atop the Palais de l'Électricité. This building, lit up with five thousand incandescent electric bulbs, became the focal point of the exhibition that celebrated technology and modernism. Even the Eiffel Tower updated its colour from reddish brown to bright yellow and was fitted with state-of-the-art electric lighting. It was a time of grand gestures and possibility. I once watched a school-project video of this period with my daughter that has stayed with me since. What would it be like to live in an age of possibility, of unfettered imagination, of expectations so great that you would build a train that travelled above the sea? Was it possible for people to appreciate that this time was special, or would it be only later, when entrenched in the Great War, that they would look back longingly? We are living in an age of anxiety. Will we know it as anything other, will we recognize an uplift when it comes our way?

⁂

A few months ago I read *A Time of Gifts* by Patrick Leigh Fermor, a travel book written about the time, at age eighteen in the 1930s, he set out to walk across Europe equipped with a walking stick, a rucksack, and a diary. As travel writer Jan Morris writes in the introduction, "the 1930s were a remembering time, and a waiting time too." This book reflects "at once the maturing of a mind and the condition of the continent."

As I got further into the Leigh Fermor book, I realized that I was waiting for him to board a train or a coach—the idea of walking across Europe unthinkable to me. But as he described rambling along desolate roads, wandering into villages, I saw that he was indeed on foot, and planned to remain so.

Once, on his way to a village, he got lost in a snowstorm, fell into a ditch and staggered into a field until he came upon a barn, where he sat huddled in layers of clothes, arms flapping occasionally to keep warm. "There was nothing for it but to sit clenched and shivering in this prehistoric burial posture and listen to my teeth rattling," he writes. Then a voice from outside, then another; villagers returning home. He looked out to see two blurs in the distance; in a moment he was rescued and five minutes later he was warm inside the local inn, listening to the strange dialect of the region.

It takes some thinking to place myself in a world where walking across Europe would be desirous. The long stretches that would have nothing to offer a traveller except boredom, discomfort, or in some cases despair, seem a case against. Would travellers be assured of a place to sleep, a place to eat? But it is in these in between places, in the nothingness that allows us to wander in eye and mind, that revelations or epiphanies are born. And trains in our age carry this stigma (or gift) of slowness, something that we can't anticipate, and the benefit of an unthinking mind, one that's allowed to be free from its moorings.

In our backyard at the height of the pandemic lockdown, I would sit in the playhouse that I called my summerhouse. I undertook the building project fifteen years ago, with no carpentry experience, and a decision to use reclaimed wood that almost undermined the whole thing. It was my daughter's place of imagination and she used it far longer than I'd expected, but she had well and truly outgrown it a few years ago. A coat of paint, spiders brushed away, a rug, a narrow set of discarded shelves, and a chair transformed it to a small study that I could use over the warm months.

When I am sitting at the back of it (out of sight, or so I believe), my view is almost panoramic as I look out into the trees, the sparse grass, and struggling perennials that make up our fully shaded backyard. The ring of trees around the boundary has made it forest dim, the strands of sunlight that break through illuminating the yard with chaotic flashes here and there.

Although I am thinking about trains, my summerhouse brings to mind a stagecoach. It is snug. I sense the outdoors keenly when I'm inside—a cooling breeze, a mosquito, a wasp, one day a bee. When I open the window I feel the sun's striated beam warm my back. This connection to nature is one I welcomed during this period, one I worked hard to attain, if only in our backyard.

On this day, knowing I will not make the journey on the Ocean, I think of the last stretch of the train ride to Moncton, the route through New Brunswick, which is largely defined by trees. Some stations, such as Jacquet River, the small village where my grandparents raised their family of eight before moving to Moncton to allow them a better education, are barely visible. Unless you happen to be in the car that stops in front of the white wooden structure, you might think the train has had a mechanical failure or is waiting for yet another freight train with its right of way on these tracks. You look out the window and see nothing but trees, then a few minutes later the train slowly makes its way to running speed. Though running speed in parts of New Brunswick is more coasting speed, and I've been told by one of the attendants that the tracks don't allow a faster pace in these parts. Upgrades are needed, and until then they have been given the go-slow order.

As we approach Moncton I am aware of how disconnected I feel to this place where I was born but left at eighteen. My family is here, of course, and I come back at least once or twice a year, but my sense of belonging to the physical space, the landscape, the culture has diminished. How we connect to the places in which we live is something I've long considered, never assuming that "home" means one thing. I've come to realize that I travel to understand the idea of home, and that this doesn't have to be one place, one connection.

❦

"There will be no travel books for the next few years," pronounced one of the presenters on the *New York Review of Books* podcast early in the pandemic. No travel, to this person, means nothing to write about.

But a travel book is never just about the trip, it is how we experience it, a way of seeing. Jan Morris refers to Patrick Leigh Fermor as "not only remembering himself but looking at himself too, as in one of those Cubist paintings in which we see profile and front face at the same time."

The Year *of*
No Travel

It is not I who has sprained my ankle,
Mademoiselle! It is the train who has sprained
my ankle. I hold none of you at fault!

—Hercule Poirot in Agatha Christie's
Murder on the Orient Express

The woman whose place we were to rent in Paris contacts me to ask whether, after this terrible year, we would be visiting her city. I look online at the pictures of her Paris residence, a former artist's house that has book-filled shelves, an outdoor courtyard, walls with musical instruments and cooking utensils and posters. This is a house I long to visit, and I have pictured myself making coffee and looking out the large windows that overlook her small garden. In some way I have already been there, having imagined myself visiting a local shop for bread, eating in a nearby restaurant, the excitement of searching for a place suitable for our group of five, that twinge of fulfillment that comes with planning travel.

In the first year of our plague I started cancelling trips. Some were small journeys—Rochester, Detroit. Others were longer—England, Spain, Paris. As it happened, I had a lot planned that year. Soon after the trips tumbled one by one into my cancellation folder, I started planning more. To actually book anything would be a folly.

Not long after, I started thinking about trips that I'd done in the past as a way of filling a longing I felt. It became a sort of mind-travelling. I was thinking specifically of trips I'd made by train because for a long time I'd been thinking of how this way of travelling, now often sidelined for the faster airplane, or the more flexible car, was the one that not only got me to where I wanted to be but added to my mental wellbeing in ways other forms didn't. And I'm a sucker for the long, lonesome wail of the train whistle.

I've been to Paris a few times, the first marked with the police clearing the airport just after I'd arrived in order to conduct a controlled explosion of an abandoned suitcase. I was looking forward to going back, to see what had actually changed—Notre Dame for certain—and what had remained locked as a permanent image—the Eiffel Tower, the River Seine, no doubt. I wanted to insert new images into this memory bank.

We bring our own consciousness, our own slant, to every new landscape we encounter, so that in thinking about a journey we are looking at it through this bias, and then in rec-reating the experience by writing about it, it becomes rewritten into our memory. This is what I decided I would do. I would rewrite these journeys to create new impressions. I could look back on past trips and think about them through the long lens of time, examine who I was then, and perhaps who I am now. I could live vicariously off my own memory of trips past. So, in the time of our plague, which was the time of no travel, this is what I would do. I would journey without leaving home.

In the opening pages of *A Journal of a Plague Year*, Daniel Defoe writes of "the last great visitation in 1665," when throngs of people were reported to be leaving London, cartloads of goods, women, children, horsemen hauling wagons loaded with baggage and fitted out for travelling. They were leaving to go to the countryside, only able to do so with a certificate of health obtained by the lord mayor that would allow them to travel through towns, to stay at inns. This exodus continued through the next few months with growing intensity when it was rumoured that the city would soon be cut off, that barriers would be put on the roads to prevent people from taking the plague with them to the outlying towns.

Defoe was just five years old at the time of the plague, so any memory he had of the event must surely have been slender at best. His writing about it would have required a great act of imagination. The title claims it was written by a citizen who was in London at the time, but the memory of the narrator is most likely taken from the journals of an uncle. In writing the book, Defoe was imagining himself into the experience.

Defoe had put himself into a different sort of adventure with the book he is most remembered for, *Robinson Crusoe*, which was published three years earlier in 1719. This account of a man who lived alone on an uninhabited island off the coast of America was also written as a "true account," and many readers believed Crusoe to be a real person, especially as the original title concludes with "written by himself." The novel was just getting started as a form, and Defoe was probably trying to give his work some legitimacy by posing it as non-fiction. He is assumed to have been inspired by the adventures of Scottish privateer Alexander Selkirk, but the book is an act of imagination. Striking out into the territory of inventiveness, he would have had to mentally put himself on that ship, and then on that island, then tell the story of this journey and how Crusoe survived. He would have had to be there without having visited anything like the deserted island that is the location. He would have had to "travel" without leaving his home.

And so I began forming my own imaginative journeys— examining past memories, conjuring future destinations. Am I ever really here, I wonder? I have tried to be present and content in my everyday life, but I know that this is only possible when there is the likelihood of going somewhere. I can only be here when I know that one day I will be somewhere else.

In revisiting these journeys, I've been scraping the thin layers of my memory to piece together what I might have said to a woman on one trip who complained about not being able to smoke on the train just after a suicide had taken place, how I felt meeting that old man who talked to me in the market square in Nuremberg all those years ago, how frightened I was when that hand reached out to grab my leg that night in the overnight couchette to Paris. I was not only writing myself into these journeys, I was reuniting with the characters involved— was I upset at the callousness of the smoking woman, would he know that I'd thought of his kindness later, that man in the square. Did I utter a word as I pulled my leg away on the train?

Some of these details I only remembered in the telling, starting off with a small image, or brief encounter, then immersing myself to explore who I was at that time of my life. It turns out there was a time I travelled alone quite a bit, and though that was due to circumstances—either because I did not have a partner or friends who were available to travel at that time—it was not something that encumbered me. There was never a question of not travelling.

***

Deborah Levy, in her book *Real Estate*, writes about her desire to acquire a grand old house, one that might have a fountain in the courtyard, the fantasy later changed to a river on the edge of the property. The dream of owning this house of her imagination follows her as she travels to New York to unpack her stepmother's apartment and to Mumbai, where she attends a literary festival, and where she visits the home of a famous architect whose stunning house leaves her cold, the water feature driving her mad with its steady, constant trickle. We are also taken to Berlin, London, Greece. This fantasy of real estate is a balm for her as she prepares for her daughter's upcoming departure to university, when she will be alone in her London apartment—her only property besides an e-bike.

I understand how this alternative reality as mansion owner soothed Levy, even when she knew on some level that this acquisition would never come to fruition. All her female friends, it seemed, were talking about their second homes, so why couldn't she do the same? She was constructing this home in her mind, an exercise that allowed her to explore what its ownership would mean to her. There was no thought of how it would be made possible.

I was having my own fantasies. It was inevitable that in thinking of trips past, I would think about the future. So while Levy dreams of real estate I thought of places I might go. This hypothetical travel was a salvation for me, especially on those days when I would feel a rising panic from thinking I would never be able to go anywhere again.

A train trip! This, our friends in England said, would give us all something to look forward to. We would do a trip across Europe when this was over, have a rail pass trip with our teenagers while they were still teenagers. And like that it moved from idea to plan. In some ways, it's as if it's already happened, like that cancelled trip to Paris. In moments of mind-travelling I am on the platform of some unnamed European city, I am reading my book on a train with one eye drifting out to take note of a French village, I am ordering a frothy coffee in some cobblestoned square. I have entered the space of this trip. I am both there and not there.

I realized as I read Levy's book that envy started creeping in, not because I yearned for my own mansion, but that in telling her story she is criss-crossing around Europe and my focus swerved so that it was these journeys and not the mansion that start to preoccupy me. There was a time I lived there and such journeys were possible. To jump on a train and visit a friend a few hours away in a different country barely required any thought or planning.

But envy soon gave way to a kind of questioning, that of what kind of traveller I was really. When Levy travels to Mumbai for the literary festival, she takes with her a turmeric-coloured silk sheet that she'd bought some time ago when she became obsessed with owning silk sheets. Now she wants to transform the sheets into a suit for herself, engaging the services of a local tailor to do so. With the help of a local friend, they leave the air-conditioned hotel and scramble around the market stalls in search of the tailor. He is found, she is measured, and he instructs her to return on Tuesday.

Having a silk suit made from your sheets might not be considered an adventure, but there was something in that act that spoke to a kind of inventiveness, or boldness, that a true traveller needs.

⁂

I am a ritual traveller, that is, one who returns to the same place again and again. I have done the same train trip on the Ocean for years, returned to Spain for over a decade; I am the type who will go to the same restaurant twice, maybe even order the same dish. There is a comfort in the familiarity of a revisited place, while it still offers the chance of small discoveries. If I know a place well enough, I can settle down to see things more clearly. It is not for me to be continually seeking novelty.

Perhaps it was enough just to be on these journeys, to have few expectations and allow myself to take in what was offered. There is a kind of existential relief when I relax into a trip with my bag of clothes and another full of books, or notes from whatever I'm working on. I can write on trains, in cars—a kind of stillness takes over that allows creative thought to flourish. I am not alone in finding literary inspiration when travelling. Stefan Zweig, in his years crossing Europe by train in the early twentieth century, created a kind of home in his compartment, one that allowed him to write, to think, to break free from the ties and habits of his life. Only then, he knew, could we not only discover the exterior world but understand the one that lives within us.

꒦꒷

The journeys on the Ocean I have taken with my daughter at the end of the school year—the twenty-seven hours by train to the east coast—hold the story of our bond. It was a ritual that allowed me to see her out of her element, watch her growing maturity, experience unfettered time alone with her. For her, it was an entry into an adult world that allowed adventure with an eye to independence. It marked a separation from the busyness of the previous few months, and allowed a kind of returning to our daydreaming selves. I would sit for hours looking out the window, observing the landscape, but thinking, too, letting my mind wander to a book I'm working on, an idea I want to pursue.

In reading of Mary Wollstonecraft's journey to Sweden, recounted in her *Letters Written During a Short Residence in Sweden, Norway, and Denmark* (1796), we witness a journey that had taken her across a "boisterous" sea to be met by curious locals—curious because they didn't get many visitors in that region, and curious because she was a woman travelling alone. We also see a woman thinking as well as observing. This was what she expected of travel, a time that gave her an opportunity to reflect, to ask questions of herself. It offered her space to explore her own thoughts and emotions, the new landscape almost a prompt by which to do so. Almost immediately upon arriving she regrets that she did not take her infant daughter with her, separated from her for the first time. Wollstonecraft is both there in Scandinavia and back in England with her child, pondering Mary's fate. In a letter written at the time she went so far as to project the future of her daughter's wellbeing, reflecting on the "dependent and oppressed state of her sex."

Already, though barely arrived, she has taken us into the deep interiority of her mind as she settles into this place. The exterior unfolds for her as she observes her surroundings; she describes the keen helpfulness of the locals, their protective nature towards the new visitor. At the same time she is "musing almost to madness" about her daughter.

But what she does observe is the beauty of her surroundings—the Norwegian horses that are stouter than English ones and do not tire easily, the fertile land, the quality of the roads the farmers are obliged to maintain. She travels to the nearest town, a distance of three Norwegian miles, which, she learns are longer than Swedish miles.

Having settled into the home of her host family, there is a return to her interior journey as she considers the landscape and the impact of the nature she has seen. She reflects on the strong impressions such beauty can have and how these scenes have become etched into her imagination: "I cannot, without a thrill of delight, recollect views I have seen, which are not to be forgotten . . . even when gazing at these tremendous cliffs, sublime emotions absorb my soul."

Wollstonecraft understood that to travel was not just to see the sights, but to examine how we feel in this new place, and that our minds, unleashed from the routine of life, are free to roam in a way not possible when thinking about what to make for dinner. In her view, "the art of travel is only a branch of the art of thinking."

With this book, Wollstonecraft broke new ground, creating a narrative that was part travelogue, part memoir. She had found a way to engage with her new surroundings that allowed her to be part of it, her own emotions, impressions, failings, disappointments laid bare. It is this interior journey that seems the signature quality of the few travel books I've read by women, until recently a rare find.

I thought of Wollstonecraft and her new way of writing about travel as I contemplated leaping into this quixotic project. How could I recreate my experiences and conjure up what I was thinking at the time? I had no journals of these trips, so I could only rely on stray impressions and the inconsistent memories I was able to harvest. It is the exterior versus the interior that I was interested in. How to describe what I saw so that I could understand how it affected me.

I wanted to understand the existential element to travel—we notice things differently, we have time to muse, to woolgather, and something in us changes.

❧

When I first started travelling to Spain I would drag and drop the little yellow man on the Google Earth map to the place I would be renting and suddenly the street image would appear. In this way I would go up the streets and my arrival would begin. I would feel the heat of the dry sun, feel the crust of the stone wall, feel the calm of the blue tiles, and in so doing I could feel my own heart slow to a pace that allowed me to take all this in. This is the traveller as observer, and as I went up and down those Google streets, I was trying to get a feel for the place, to see the terrain. Sometimes I zoomed in to see the detail of the village square, or the type of shop on the corner near the house where I'd be staying. Curiosity was the driver here; I was not seeking any practical information.

The anthropologist Margaret Mead's entire professional career relied on travel and observation. Her life's work was that of recording far-off cultures, some of which would rarely be visited by anyone else. She viewed the local culture with the understanding that every small detail was significant and indicative of who they were as a whole. In writing about her work, she speaks of the role of the anthropologist to do consciously what "the young child, filled with boundless energy and curiosity, does without conscious purpose—that is learn about a whole world." Can we as travellers learn to see the place we visit in this manner, without expectation or judgment?

Mead refers to this process of observation as an "active waiting, a readiness in which all his senses are alert to whatever may happen, expected or unexpected, in the next five minutes—or in an hour, a week, or a month from now." To have our senses so alive and alert, surely this is the way we should live.

What would she have thought of my Google map travelling? I suspect she would be bemused by it. As someone whose life was dedicated to experiential travel, this form of virtual travel would likely have seemed fraudulent. But during the pandemic this is all I had. That and the travel memoirs and books on the social history of trains stacked on my shelves. In thinking of those past trips, I relied on these virtual maps to take me back to places like that Nuremberg square where that kind old man bought me a beer and showed me the good luck charm in a nearby market square fountain. The online picture of the fountain does not spark my memory, in fact I barely recognize it as the fountain that I walked up to and where I rubbed the brass ring that held the promise of luck. I can only see this detail, my hand reaching out, stroking the ring, then walking away to allow the next seeker to have a go. Of all that I experienced that day in Nuremberg it is the sensory detail of that ring that stands out, the memory branded so that I can be there long after I've left.

In a year and a half when I might have travelled thousands of miles, I did not leave a radius of more than a hundred miles. I don't know when last I could say such a thing. It is a given that I missed my family and my friends, and both require lengthy travel to see them. I was anxious, edgy, constantly making plans for future trips then stopping myself when I remembered that the time of no travel had moved on to the time of no plans.

No, I tell the woman in Paris, I won't be visiting your beautiful home this year. In fact, I didn't know when I would get there. I remained on my porch, or in my daughter's playhouse reclaimed as my summerhouse, or working from the spare room that is now my office, letting my mind wander to far-off places. Those cancelled trips will ease back into my life eventually, and I'm looking ahead to a train trip in Europe with friends now full of possibility as each of us claims our favourite destination—Venice, Poland, Greece. But, until then I wait.

Uncoupling

*I don't belong to this railway journey at all—I
was in a wood just now—and I wish I could get
back there!*

—Alice in Lewis Carroll's
Through the Looking-Glass

In my memory we were in the shadows. The flecks of reflected light from the streetlights made silhouettes of us inside the compartment. Were there more than just us two in that compartment? I don't remember. But eventually we were alone, this German man and I, and the conversation began as such things do: stilted, polite, mildly curious.

It was the darkness I remember. This night train from Nuremberg to Warsaw revealed nothing of the landscape outside the city. I was relieved to be on my way back, after having talked my way into a lift to Munich with Piotr, a Polish work colleague, a trip that went classically awry. Though I had a few friends in Warsaw, none were able to travel to Germany for the weekend and I really wanted to get away. The women in my office were single and had a good income, but it was not their habit to travel like this, alone with another woman. Piotr worked in the ministry office, a low-level job that suited his long hair and poetic nature. He was going to Munich to visit friends. I was going as far as he would take me.

We'd travelled from Warsaw in his Fiat 126, a model affectionately referred to as "maluch," or little one, by the Poles who drove them. The car was tiny and finicky, and there were problems with the engine somewhere near the Polish border. Our unplanned overnight stay upended the one plan I had made—grabbing a lift to another city for the weekend.

The car breakdown meant it was now too far to travel in the short time I had off work, and so on a whim I had Piotr drop me off in Nuremberg. All I knew of the city was the trials. But I was not there to look into its past, having had no intention of going there at all. I was alone in a place I hadn't planned on visiting.

There was a small inn at the edge of the old town where I secured an attic room with slanted ceilings. I bought food and ate it in my room, overcome with a swift feeling of abandonment after having come so far with Piotr, mixed with a sense of great accomplishment in finding a room so late. Sometimes there are small joys in travel that can barely be counted.

The next day I met an elderly man in the Hauptmarkt, a large outdoor market where I'd found a table, something to eat, a place to rest. I had spent the day walking, taking in the atmosphere of the city, leaving the historic sites to the tourists. It was late afternoon, the sun was out, and after we'd talked for some time the man insisted on buying me a wheat beer. I had never heard of such a thing. When we'd finished we walked over to Schöner Brunnen, a gothic, fourteenth-century

fountain that stands almost thirty feet tall. Forty colourful figures adorn the fountain, representing religious and allegorical
characters of the Holy Roman Empire.

You should turn it, my new friend said when he led me to a
brass ring on the fence that surrounds the fountain. It is said to
bring good luck to those who do so. The legend goes that the
ring was inserted by a journeyman who had fallen in love with
his master's daughter. She returned his love, but the master
would not allow them to get married. While the master and
daughter were away on a trip, the journeyman made the ring
and inserted it in the railing seamlessly. He then left Nuremberg
in despair. When the master returned and saw the ring, he was
impressed and tried to find the young man who had such skill
but it was too late, he could not find him anywhere. From that
time onward, it's said for those who rotate the ring and make a
wish, it will come true.

When I stood too long at the ring, rotating it slowly, with
intent, my friend asked why I needed so much good luck.

❧

This is what I remember of the trip. The market, the kind man
who spoke to me, then introduced me to wheat beer, and the
lucky fountain. Why does our memory sift through events and
leave so many holes? How does memory work in a place like
Nuremberg, the world stage for war crimes? There was no
precedent for these international trials that would set the path
for the Geneva Convention. This one would bring together
two judges from each of four countries: Britain, France, the
Soviet Union, and the United States, establishing the laws and

procedures necessary to conduct the trials in three categories: crimes against peace, war crimes, and crimes against humanity.

Along with the legal entanglement of having four countries in charge of the trials, there was the issue of four languages to deal with. Although taken for granted today, simultaneous translation was unheard of then and IBM had to bring in special equipment, and people were recruited from international telephone exchanges to do on-the-spot translation. The city of Nuremberg was selected because its Palace of Justice remained relatively undamaged by the war and it had a large prison. Also the city itself had hosted annual Nazi propaganda rallies, so having the trials there was symbolic.

There were thirteen Nuremberg Trials between 1945 and 1949; the first and most famous tried the major war criminals. That trial, for the direct perpetrators of the Holocaust, took a year, then an American tribunal tried doctors for their medical experiments, lawyers and judges for implementing the eugenics laws, industrialists accused of using slave labour, and SS officers for violence against concentration camp inmates.

For this first trial, the tribunal found all but three of the twenty-four defendants, including Hermann Göring and Rudolf Hess, guilty. Twelve were sentenced to death, and the rest were given prison sentences of ten years to life.

<hr />

I didn't know the details of the trials when I visited there, nor did I know about the hangman, Master Sergeant John C. Woods, whose photos on the Internet invariably show him gripping a noose, and who is reported to have botched the job on each execution. Those convicted died of slow strangulation rather than a quick snap of the neck. Of this he is reported to have said to a group of war correspondents, "I hanged those ten Nazis . . . and I am proud of it . . . I wasn't nervous. . . . A fellow can't afford to have nerves in this business."

When I visited the Auschwitz concentration camp some months later, I no longer remember if Nuremberg was specifically on my mind. I took the train from Warsaw to Kraków, then a bus to the camp. That day was grey; it may have been misting, and as we walked around from building to building, it was hard to connect the things we were seeing to the activity we knew had taken place. We knew what the pile of children's shoes represented, but the level of human suffering is beyond imagination, even when given such ghastly evidence.

Photos of the train tracks with the watchtower in the background have become iconic. The tracks are loomed over by the watchtower, the end station that the estimated 1.3 million would not have seen as they arrived at the camp, crowded as they were into windowless cars. The watchtower, however, would become the unnerving eye monitoring their movement every day they remained alive. This image of the tracks and the tower is what most of us recognize of Auschwitz. But what we don't see is the other perspective, the direction from which the trains have come. This is the outbound view, one that would represent escape, a vast nothingness of fields and trees. The image from one perspective representing terror, the other freedom. That, along with the shoes, is a memory that lingers.

In recent years there has been a trend among those visiting of taking selfies at Auschwitz. Some walk those train tracks to get the tower in the background, then pose as if they are in a fashion shoot. The need for evidence of their being there overrides any respect for this terrible moment in history. I've seen this at the 9/11 memorial site in New York as well, people taking pictures of their smiling children in front of the place that honours one of the most devastating events of our lifetime. Some people don't understand the difference between a memorial site and a tourist attraction, my husband noted as we watched people holding smart phones in the air, smiling. The farther we get from the event, the less horror memory holds.

On my way to Auschwitz, sitting on that bus to Oświęcim, the town now famed for having this most notorious concentration camp, I chatted to Judith, whom I'd met and befriended at a conference in Holland the year before. There were others travelling with us, a reunion of sorts of those who'd attended that conference. Judith and I were deep in conversation when another in our group, a woman who, we came to realize, had relatives killed during the Holocaust, reached across the aisle, her hand resting on Judith's arm. Please stop talking, she said, indicating that we would soon be there. We knew this woman to be forthright by nature—it was not a surprising request—but still we felt the sting of being scolded. We obeyed, of course, turning to look out the window, to see the innocuous countryside that surrounded the camp. She was right, I would realize later, to quieten us, not just in respect for her own mourning, but to remind us that we were entering a space where reverence was needed. We couldn't just barge in with our gossipy chatter, we needed time to adjust our mental space so that we could really understand why we were there, and why its history had made it notorious. It was an important lesson I may have begrudged at the time, but it did make me think about the fact that I was there to honour the memory of the Holocaust rather than consume the place as a tourist destination. And that this honouring required me to go through the camp slowly and in silence.

❧

I learned later that Nuremberg has a significant history that predates the trials. It is also known as the place where many of the racial laws that codified Nazi ideology came into being at a 1935 rally. The Nuremberg Race Laws, influenced by American race law, were devised after Nazi lawyers researched Jim Crow laws in America to determine how they had subjugated African Americans. According to James Q. Whitman in his book *Hitler's American Model: The United States and the Making of Nazi Race Law*, "Nazi lawyers regarded America, not without reason, as the innovative world leader in racist law." The Nuremberg Race Laws would deny Jews German citizenship and provide the framework for their systematic persecution.

Much of this history of Nuremberg, I discovered more recently. Then, I simply tromped around and after three days took the overnight train back to Warsaw. Despite the long journey I purchased a ticket for a compartment seat, not a sleeper. The night glistened outside my window, the streets perpetually damp at this time of year. I had not spoken to anyone aside from the man in the market, the one who gave me the gift of luck. I was used to travelling alone, used to keeping to myself, and it felt like a form of luck that I fell into an easy conversation with the German man, the other occupant in the compartment. Since it was too early for sleep, we talked, and the hours rolled by and the intimacy of this encounter deepened so that neither of us sought sleep. It seemed as though all my melancholic wanderings in Nuremberg had prepared me for this intense moment of connection, the entire trip leading to this. Where are you from, where are you going? We would hasten those questions and talk of our lives—the story of why I had ended up in Poland, his family in Berlin—words spread out before us in that confined space, an instant familiarity. Had we known each other before? He remains with me still, that stranger on a train. The abiding memory of this trip is not the history of the city that I am now piecing together to get a better understanding of the place I'd been, but the kindness of the man in the market, the connection to this one on the train.

Travel gives us a sense of forgetting about our lives and its incumbrances and offers the possibility of renewal. I went to Nuremberg because I was lonely. It made me feel reckless in a way I needed, of being carefree enough to go, and it gave me a sense of control over my life. I was working in a highly patriarchal, post-Communist environment, returning each night to an empty flat. I needed to recapture the sense of independence I once knew. I didn't need to make plans with others, to rely on others. I would travel alone, hitch a ride, take the train back. Easy. Solo travelling was not new to me, but there was a desperation I felt this time. I'd been through a bad patch and it was as though I needed to remind myself to live fully, and the first step would be to go somewhere, create my own adventure. It was not so much that travel was a challenge for me, but that I had to overcome the obstacles I'd set myself.

In *The Virago Book of Women Travellers*, I read that the travel writer Isabella Bird (1831–1904), up to the age of forty had stayed home to care for family members and would have stayed there indefinitely if the doctors hadn't prescribed travel to cure her bad back and insomnia. This is what I had done, I thought when reading about this clever doctor's treatment, I had self-prescribed travel to cure my loneliness. I think that's why it is those two connections—the young man on the train, the old man in the market—that I remember more than anything else about the trip. Sometimes we find what we don't know we're seeking.

On that overnight train to Warsaw, an announcement blared over the loudspeaker in German, startling us from our intimacy. He jumped up, grabbed my bag, and my hand, and told me to follow him, quickly. The train would be separating, he told me, and I had to move to a car that would take me to Warsaw; he would remain on this one to Berlin. In the corridor there were lights, and people weaving past one another, the conductor directing everyone, and this stranger holding my hand to ensure I got where I needed to be. Just as there'd been a scramble when Piotr dropped me off at the beginning of the weekend, I would have another abrupt departure.

The leave-taking was swift. There was little to say. We may have kissed.

The Tedium
of Velocity

This snorting little animal which I felt rather
inclined to pat, was then harnessed to our
carriage, and, Mr Stephenson having taken
me on the bench of the engine with him, we
started at ten miles an hour. You can't imagine
how strange it seemed to be journeying on thus,
without any visible cause of progress other than
the magical machine, with its flying white breath
and rhythmical, unvarying pace.

—Fanny Kemble, a British actress who travelled
with George Stephenson, the man who built
the first steam locomotive to carry passengers
on a public line, in a letter to a friend, later
published in Kemble's *Records of a Girlhood*

I f you were to travel from the south of England to Warsaw,
Poland, by train, it would take approximately twenty-one
hours. By car, it would be seventeen hours. To fly it would
take two hours. If you had a hankering to go a slower pace, I've

calculated—because I'm interested in how a distance travelled can range from an afternoon jaunt to several weeks' commitment—that it would take 126 hours by stagecoach. This is based on the relative speed of early steam trains, which were three times as fast as the stagecoach, and assuming that modern non-highspeed trains would be at least twice that.

But this calculation is complicated by the fact that the English Channel separates England from France, so in the time of stagecoaches, a boat trip would have to be added. Already this stagecoach journey is over five days long, but this is with continuous travel, so you would have to add weeks to take into account overnight stays along the way as well.

This is not a perfect science, and it's unlikely that even if it were an option, I would opt for the stagecoach, so named because they travel in "stages" of ten or fifteen miles, and which, despite the pastoral setting in which they traversed and a cozy intimacy if travelling with agreeable passengers, were fraught with problems from highwaymen stealing your jewellery and coin to odorous travelling companions. This is my amateur attempt to do what our modern GPS does for us in an instant, determining the trip length with options for train, bus, car, and walking. Invariably we opt for the quickest, because we want to get where we are going as fast as we can. I did not calculate how long it would take to walk to Warsaw.

I had not been back to Poland for fifteen years. I'd lived there for three years at the time of my Nuremberg trip, and it felt like it was time to return, this time with my husband and daughter.

We would start from our base on Hayling Island in the south of England, and we would, of course, take the train.

When I began thinking about my re-entry into Warsaw I knew it should be slow, considered, after all this time away. That period in Poland had been an axis on which the rest of my life had pivoted, and going back would be like visiting my former self. I knew that I would need time to process what it meant to return to where I'd lived just after the fall of Communism. I had left a relationship and slipped into a new career, and then I'd left it all to go back to school in England. Flying into Warsaw would feel too abrupt, too disorienting. I'm not sure what I was expecting exactly, but I knew I needed time. Travelling by train would give me that.

❦

In the nineteenth century, writers who wrote about trains as a new form of transportation were preoccupied with time and space travelled. They wrote about the advent of trains as the annihilation of both, the way the speed of this new beast managed to shrink time so that Birmingham had become closer to London by two-thirds. This shrinking of space, which translated to time, meant that travel for ordinary people became possible. One didn't have to be wealthy with limitless free time. Before trains, those interested in faraway places would have "panoramic" or "dioramic" shows or gadgets as the only way of "visiting" them. Now that trains had brought destinations closer they could go there, experience it for themselves. Former remote places exclusive to the aristocracy now saw middle-class travellers flocking there. Tourism flourished.

Trains also forced towns and villages in England and elsewhere to abandon "local time" and adopt a uniform time so that train schedules lined up. Until then, each operated on their own clock, with London time running four minutes ahead of Reading, and seven minutes, thirty seconds ahead of Cirencester, for example. It was the railways that forced the adoption of Greenwich Mean Time in England and Standard time in the United States and Canada.

I began to stitch together the various legs to Poland to see if it were even feasible by train, and then piece by piece I started booking them. I stretched our trip even further by planning a day in Paris, followed by the overnight train to Berlin, where we would have a day there as well so, in fact, it would take nearly thirty-six hours to get there. Our trip had nothing to do with shrinking time or space, in fact we expanded it nearly twenty-fold.

The train from Hayling Island is at Havant station across a half-mile bridge to the mainland, and an hour and twenty minutes from London, so is largely for commuters. The trains are built for efficiency over comfort, with cloth-covered plastic seats and hydraulic doors, though they do have an attendant come through with a snack trolley. The train travels through bucolic English countryside, with farms and sheep and traditional stations. It is a good way to ease into our trip, watching the rising tide of people in suits heading to work in the city.

We were the only passengers in our carriage with bigger plans for the day, clutching our luggage as if declaring, or perhaps, defending, our status as travellers. I gripped our tickets, having booked each leg hoping they would all line up, that one train wouldn't be late, leaving us scrambling for the next. A travel agent might have been a good idea, but this is the age of self-directed travel so it didn't occur to me until later to consult one.

In London we had to change to a station across town and decided we couldn't risk the melee of the Underground to get from Waterloo to St. Pancras International, and so we took a black cab. This was a treat and made us feel like we were in some sort of caper as we dashed across London to catch our train to Paris.

I am thinking of that race through the station, the worry of missing our train, as I lament our pandemic-cancelled trip that would have followed the same route from Havant to Paris, this time with my family and parents-in-law. The casual mention of aborted trips became the connector in many lockdown conversations: Japan, Spain, Montreal, China, New York—the list from friends and acquaintances piled up and I became newly aware just how small the world has become. This feels like a cliché—what a small world—but it is true, our expectations to go farther, faster, is a given these days.

But things changed as almost the entire world locked down. We thought of time differently; we thought of space differently. After more than a century of technological advance in travel that saw the shrinking of space, we were now doing the opposite, we expanded it to the point where destinations couldn't be accessed at all. Some went back to slow travel, limited to taking an automobile to cottages, campsites, a hotel in a nearby city. We have been going too fast, people said, we need to slow our pace; we now need to appreciate the vistas close to us, the ones we'd overlooked, the ones that felt insignificant. Could we really do that, go back to the days when the traveller was going slow enough that their eyes would focus on a particular person, a tree, a house, so that they would examine it, consider the aesthetics, become curious or reflective? We have become too used to arriving, the journey itself so tiresome we can hardly bear it. But now we were forced again to look at our own surroundings, taking in nature, taking long walks, seeking places to eat al fresco. "The great pause," it was called.

The Eurostar was full from London, and though it was plusher and more comfortable than the last train, it seemed a bit small and I tried not to let my claustrophobia creep in. We sat at a table and played a game with our daughter, and watched more of the verdant countryside, for which England is so famous, pass by. We pointed with excitement at sheep, just as we have done when we saw cows or horses or deer on any number of other train trips. I'm not sure why we are excited to see them when we are cutting through their territory, perhaps we feel it a testament to our powers of observation. Perhaps this is a primal urge to observe our surroundings that we can trace back to an earlier time. Perhaps we just like to look at sheep.

We swept through the Kent countryside arriving at the channel tunnel, which takes twenty minutes to go through, like an extended subway, and I was awed that we could so quickly be in another country, the entry so seamless. The land in this part of France is flat and largely agricultural until we near Paris, which like any city sprawls in ways that don't add to its beauty. This train was bolting at around 180 miles per hour, though our only way of knowing this was by the swiftly moving view.

One measure of speed attributed to early trains was in relation to that of a cannonball, and in these modern times, I can't help but think of us as a bullet travelling through the space, images screeching by with no time for our eyes to focus. This was about twice the speed of trains I was used to, so we turned away from the windows to read, to play another game.

⁂

In *La bête humaine*, the 1938 film by Jean Renoir, the opening scene is of a conductor driving a steam train. He is in the roofless engine car while his fireman shovels coal into a wild blaze and there is a sense of them flying through the French countryside. The conductor frequently sticks his head out the side of the train to get a better view, and it's hard not to think of the close shaves he would have with obstacles like poles and tunnels. When he stands straight up he is facing a small window in a wall of dials, gauges, and levers. There is the steady clatter of the train on the tracks and the constant motion of hydraulics—the propulsion is intense. The conductor wears goggles and his face, as with the face of the fireman, is grime-smeared. The camera view shifts from inside the engine platform, where the two men are making adjustments, blowing the whistle, feeding the coal fire to keep the train moving, to the perspective the conductor sees outside when he leans out, or down at the level where the wheels are thrumming. There is a choreography between the two men, that of a whistle blown, or a tap on the head, or the gesture of blowing a horn as the conductor gives instruction to the fireman. The fireman has a cigarette in his mouth throughout. The movie title translates to "The Human Beast," but in the scenes where they are on the train, because most of it takes place in this engine car, it appears that this is the beast referred to—a sleek, puffing, fire-breathing animal that is working in tandem with the humans.

Watching this film, I could understand how fearsome these new "beasts" were, why they were considered the jet engines of the day, and how the term "flying" was used by nineteenth-century writers for them. In the film, the steam train thrusts through the landscape—though the average speed would have been only thirty to sixty miles per hour—and these scenes are a kind of homage to this new way of travelling. Renoir was intent on realism for this film, and it almost cost his cinematographer nephew his life when he had to cling to the train as it sped through a tunnel. (His camera did not survive the tunnel.) The film is based on a novel by Émile Zola, and was reportedly made because its star and producer Jean Gabin, an icon of French cinema, had a passion for steam trains. He is the engineer—the role of a lifetime for him.

On our highspeed train, we "flew" through the French country-side and became what the art critic John Ruskin said of travellers who took the train from Paris to the Mediterranean in the 1800s: "human parcels who dispatched themselves to their destination by means of the railroad, arriving as they left, untouched by the space traversed."

Our trip was not long enough for boredom to set in, but I could see what it might have been like for those early travellers, used to a more meditative pace. Accustomed to slowness, they could not process this shocking velocity and so, like many modern travellers, they resorted to sleep. Before any train journey, the French novelist Gustave Flaubert would stay up all night so that he could sleep through the journey, having no interest in experiencing any of it, with no desire to take in the rapidly moving view. Flaubert wrote to a friend in 1864: "I get so bored in the train that I'm about to howl with tedium after five minutes of it. One might think that it's a dog someone has forgotten in the compartment; not at all. It is M. Flaubert, groaning."

The monotony of train travel was soon alleviated with the introduction of bookstalls that began appearing in stations across England. William Henry Smith established a bookstall at Euston Station and soon had the rights to conduct business across stations in London and the Northwestern Railway. In his "Essay on London" of 1888 Henry James writes of the W. H. Smith and Son's bookstalls as "a focus of warmth and light. In the vast smoky cavern; it gives the idea that literature is a thing of splendor, of dazzling essence, of infinite gas-lit red and gold. A glamour hangs over the glittering booth, and a tantalizing air of clever new things." These stalls were set up to sell books, but they also offered a lending service. Private lending libraries were popular at the time, and in 1860 Smith added this feature. For a subscription fee you could borrow a book and return it to the station once done. The shortage of space in the stalls meant that subscribers would have to wait for the book ordered through a catalogue and delivered by train to the station the next day.

The bookstalls' influence on the publishing industry is told in a legendary story of publisher Allen Lane, who was returning home after a weekend visit with Agatha Christie and found nothing worth reading at the Exeter Station bookstall. This inspired him to set up Penguin Books to publish cheap, quality books for the masses. It's said that he later set up the nonfiction imprint and named it Pelican Books after over-hearing a woman at the Kings Cross train station asking for one of those "Pelican" books, by which she meant the familiar orange-and-white Penguins. The Pelican series, with its blue-and-white cover, was launched shortly after.

It was not just boredom and the inability to see the particulars of the outside scenery that proved a strain for early train travel-lers. The heightened level of stimulation brought about by this blur of images was exhausting. Travellers slept from boredom but also from overstimulation. In a letter dated 30 October 1873, an anonymous author wrote: "There are people, hurried by their business, who . . . in the course of one day have to cast their eyes upon the panorama of several hundreds of places. They arrive at their destination overwhelmed by a previously unknown fatigue. . . . The agitated mind has called sleep to the rescue, it puts an end to overexcitation."

We were in our own state of "overexcitation" when we arrived in Paris, the train slowing as we made our way through the industrial outskirts, the rim of residential neighbourhoods until we reached Gare du Nord, the busiest station in Europe. It was built between 1861 and 1865 in the Beaux-Arts style, with a stone facade that features twenty-three female statues, each representing a European city. I saw none of this as we stepped off the train and met our friend who spends several months annually in Paris. He would be our guide for the day so we did not have to fret about what Métro to take, or even how to get tickets. My memory of that day is reduced to flickers of us walking the city, for it seemed that the only thing we could do in the short time we had was to absorb the essence of the place.

My husband and I had been to Paris before but our daughter had not, so we wanted to show her the sights that might be recognizable to an eight-year-old. But the impressions of this day blended with other visits, and I don't know if this speaks to capacity limits in our memory banks or if it's just that the small events get crowded out by the glaringly significant. In this case the significant was the moment when, focused on conversation with our friend rather than our surroundings, we turned the corner and there before us was the Eiffel Tower. We went from the banal to the extraordinary in that moment, our daughter's face lit with awe. To witness her reaction to seeing the tower for the first time, after knowing it from souvenir trinkets or picture books, reminded us of how immune we can become to the spectacular.

It turns out the spectacular was lost on her because she has little memory of the Eiffel Tower itself, her only memory was having her picture taken in front of it. Of the city, she was only able to recall dancing by the River Seine as she ate pizza and the trouble we had finding our sleeping car later when we had to leave for Berlin.

Because I don't have a mind that intuits structural engineering, when I read about the Eiffel Tower I am struck by random details about its construction, such as the fact that it required two and a half million rivets. And that each rivet took four men to place it—one to heat it up, another to hold it in place, another to shape the head, the last to strike it with a sledgehammer. I am left wondering how many they would have installed in a day, what it would have been like for the workmen who had to breathe the heated (and probably toxic) air, and how hard on the body it would have been to endure the regular jolt of the sledgehammer. At the time of construction this would not have been work to take pride in, as leading figures from the world of arts and literature formed a protest movement against its building, calling it "useless and monstrous." Guy de Maupassant was said to have detested the tower but would eat lunch there every day. When asked why he dined there, he said it was the only place in Paris where he couldn't see it.

＊

We lingered, taking in the view, before walking to the base of the tower, stopping to buy our daughter a very expensive ice cream from a vendor nearby. Then it was time to return to the station to catch our overnight train to Berlin. We decided that our five p.m. departure meant we should buy a baguette and other supplies and have a picnic for the train. I can become obsessed with food, particularly the ritual of it, and this picnic became a fixation as we made our way to the station, with me dashing in and out of shops looking for the elusive bread. For a while it seemed that a baguette, some cheese, and wine were the only things that would make this a perfect day in Paris;

even then I was aware of the cliché I was perpetuating. But alas, it was late in the day and a baguette was not to be found, and so I was forced to settle on pastries and, once on board, a cold beer served by the attendant.

I have travelled enough to know the danger of expectations. We may form a picture in our head of what our destination will look like, what the people we encounter will be like, what we will experience. It can stir up wild disappointment when notched too high or offer sudden delight when our expectations are low or off the mark. It can affect the way you view the Eiffel Tower when you've seen it for the third or fourth time and your anticipation has been blunted by familiarity, but this time with your daughter, you see it anew. It can also trigger a mild tantrum over the failure of a perfect picnic, when really a beer and a pastry will do.

I expected to visit Paris in the summer of the first lockdown, but the travel limitations meant I couldn't. I still don't know when I'll be back, just as I couldn't make plans beyond the next week in that first summer of the pandemic. Next year, we'd say, when talking of travel plans, almost afraid of jinxing it. I hoped this year of pause would also teach us a different sort of expectation—that we would travel better, do better in much of the way that we live when normal life returned. Patience became the lesson, as we sat in our homes gazing out into a life that might once again include dinner with friends, a flight to a foreign city, a holiday with family. We could not have thought this an eventuality in our lives, that we would be so restricted. This constant threat of illness, of becoming infected or infecting others ruled our lives. It was not war, but some likened the experience of it to the threat and limitation experienced in times of conflict. Or of past pandemics we only knew from history books. Never had we felt so little control over our lives.

What will we learn, what lessons will stay with us? We had not been doing well for a long time, it seems. The year of pause was also the year of calamity as we dealt with racial reckoning, threats to democracy, and the climate crisis in the background of the pandemic.

I fear that we have learned nothing in the end. But it is still too soon to know for sure. What we need is time, the great informant, to really know what lies ahead. For me, I've learned that Paris can wait.

The top bunk of our three-tiered cabin from Paris to Berlin was a coffin-like space that my husband claimed by default—too high for our daughter, too closed in for me. Next door was a mother, father, teenage son, and their dog. The presence of the dog impressed me. It was a reminder that these cabins were more affordable than I'd expected, and therefore aimed at all manner of travellers who wanted to sleep well on this over-night leg, families and dogs included, and not priced as luxury accommodations like some other railways.

The attendant came and offered us cold Heineken and returned swinging the bottles between his fingers, with a juice for our daughter. He asked if we needed anything else before dashing off to get the next order. There may have been safety regulations and instructions recited at some point, but the fact that he was like a good host, focussing on our comfort and, more important, our thirst was the thing I remembered.

We sat on the bottom bunk still set up as a seat, our baggage on the floor, no room to move without crawling over one another, and took out our food; we would have our picnic after all. To be in such cramped space after roaming Paris was to return to nesting, and it settled my restlessness, allowing for a moment of contentment. We were there together, within reach. The three of us, introverts, each lost somewhere in our own ruminations, alone together.

There is a bit of playing house in this scenario, though perhaps it's more the joy of absconding from the duties of our everyday lives. I'm reminded of the feeling I get when camping, that point at which the three of us would climb into the tent, slip into our sleeping bags, reach for our books, our bodies falling into each other as we clumsily settled in.

We left Paris much as we leave any city, through changing neighbourhoods, our eyes on the way people live—a woman clutching bags from shopping, a child running down the sidewalk, laundry hanging from a balcony—and soon we were in the industrial wasteland, and then the countryside. We viewed this through our lozenge-shaped window, each of us taking a turn for a better view. We created our own world, sealed up in our chamber. When dusk came we lost interest in the passing tableaux and reached for pyjamas, books, toothbrushes. Soon we were stacked in our beds, with nightlight and book in hand, and soon after we were asleep because it had been a full day, and the swaying, oh the swaying, soothed us to sleep.

We were roused to an alarm in the morning, which we soon realized was our wake-up call. We would be in Berlin in the next hour or so and must get up, dress, and have the breakfast they prepared for us. We had slept well, wrapped in our white cotton sheets, our heads on soft pillows, and one by one we occupied the only floor space where we could stand amidst our bags to dress. The family with the dog next door was no longer there and their cabin beds had been converted back to chairs so the attendant let us eat our breakfast in there. The breakfast tray was like those on planes and as it was unexpected it felt like a treat. We had yogurt, fruit, and a pastry with our juice and coffee so we were set, which was good because, as the train sauntered into Berlin, it dawned on us that we would disembark at a station on the outskirts, and not at the central train station we had expected, where our train to Warsaw was to depart later that day. We were left at an abandoned platform and our attempt to get help from the few passengers was hindered by our lack of German, their lack of English. Eventually we were led to a commuter train that took us to the Berlin Central Station, a sleek glass-and-steel building, the insides of which resembled a shopping mall.

In the hours between trains, we left our bags at the station and walked to the Reichstag, home of the German parliament. An elegant building with expansive green space in front, it was difficult for me to separate it from its connection to Hitler. The Reichstag Fire of 1933 was seen as the pivotal moment in Hitler's rise to power, when, as chancellor, his accusations that this fire was the work of the Communists prompted President Hindenburg to invoke Article 48, allowing for executive orders. The act abolished freedom of speech, assembly, privacy, and the press, and legalized phone tapping and interference of correspondence. To this day, the term "Reichstag Fire" remains a political metaphor for a cautionary tale against executive overreach.

It was difficult to explain to our daughter why those in power felt it necessary to build a wall to separate people. As we walked the five minutes from the Reichstag to the Brandenburg Gate, my husband, an historian, attempted to do so. We tried to impress upon her the swift and unexpected turn that history took in the fall of the Berlin Wall—one of those events where those who were old enough remember where they were when hearing the news. I grew up in era where nuclear war was a likely event and the Iron Curtain as real as the draperies in my parents' home, so this news was world changing. But our daughter didn't understand the impact of the "after," as she was not there for the "before." She had not held the belief as we did that this Wall would be forever, and so in the telling of this story, I was aware that for her it was just another moment, as was World War II, as were all the other moments that changed and evolved and became something heard about rather than something real and lived.

Recently we three listened to *Tunnel 29*, a podcast documentary about a group of people who came together to build a tunnel between East and West Germany in the early sixties, and helped twenty-nine people escape. The podcast reminded us of that day in Berlin and it gave us extra insight into the experience of the people we were hearing about. It's hard to know how much our daughter remembers of our short stop in Berlin, or how much she absorbed later through her own interest in World War II history. For me, visiting the Brandenburg Gate was significant because of my time in post-Communist Poland, knowing people who were directly affected by the Wall. I remember one of the students to whom I taught English telling the story of visiting Brussels not long after the Wall came down, standing in front of a candy store weeping, overwhelmed by the opulence and abundance.

But the Brandenburg Gate is, in the end, like any memorial, a place of the imagination. We stood among other tourists, looking at this neoclassical structure built in the eighteenth century, and we tried to erase the modern throng around us to imagine the barren road, the ever-watching soldiers, the fear of even thinking to cross this border.

Later we waited under the hulking glass dome at Berlin Central Station, sitting on our bags, eager for this last train that would take us to Warsaw. When it arrived, on time with a newness and efficiency that matched the station, we joined the small crowd boarding the train. Our business-class seats, bought because these tickets were still quite cheap, were at a table of four in a car with only another table for two, next to the kitchen. It felt spacious, though it was also a throughway. The crew were speaking Polish. This, I hadn't expected, and it reminded me of the purpose of the trip.

Soon we were in the Polish hinterland, and it appeared as though modernity had not found these villages and hamlets, despite the fall of the Wall. Plaster-clad houses with crumbling facades, shops with faded signs, years-old cars that were for function rather than flash—a true sign of poverty in a country where BMWs and Mercedes had quickly become the badge of wealth in the early open-market days. This was a sharp contrast to what I would see in our three days in Warsaw visiting my former work colleague Klaus and his wife, Gosia. In the city where I once worked, I would see designer shops and restaurants and foreign cars, a café society as in any Western city. I would see wealth in great contrast to the poverty we saw on our train trip to get there, and it would make me wonder what had really changed in all the years I'd been away. Authoritarians had simply been replaced by oligarchs, it seemed.

꘎

When it was time to eat we were confused by the dinner menu on the train and ordered too much. We ended up with a small buffet on our table, some things barely touched. We were embarrassed when the attendant asked if we were finished. I had started to teach my daughter some of the Polish I remembered, and she laughed when I told her the word for "yes" is "tak."

Tak, tak, tak, she said over and over, like it was a word game we were playing.

The businessman across the aisle smiled at her charm, and outside I could see the first lights of Warsaw in the darkness. I stood at the window for a while, my daughter announcing, "Mama's getting excited." I don't know if I was excited, my feelings a jumble as I considered what it was that I was anticipating in this return. As we reached our thirty-sixth hour of travelling, we pulled into the city I'd once known and now in darkness could not see. Soon we would be in the station, and we gathered our bags. The train entered the tunnel-like station, the doors opened, and the familiar smell of cold concrete hit me.

The Grand Tour

*Nothing can be more unpresuming than this little
volume. It contains the account of some desultory
visits by a party of young people to scenes which
are now so familiar to our countrymen, that few
facts relating to them can be expected to have
escaped the many more experienced and exact
observers, who have sent their journals to the press.*

—Percy Bysshe Shelley, preface of *History of
a Six Weeks' Tour* by Mary Shelley

I see us sprawled on the lawn of the château, our bicycles
resting nearby. Our bags are carelessly tossed to one side, and
there are wrappers for the baguette and cheese we'd had for
lunch. We are happy drunk, tired, and only mildly conscious of
the fact that sixteen miles out means sixteen miles back. We'd
mustered courage to stop at the vineyards because they seemed
less like commercial enterprises, more like being invited into a
local farmhouse. This was France; I was twenty-five and the

authenticity I was in search of in this first trip to Europe had manifested itself in the form of a country winery.

We'd been in Paris the day before, and the next day we'd go to Tours, or perhaps Angers; we'd yet to decide, our destination a whim based on the train schedule. It was my friend's idea to visit towns and hire bikes to explore France; it was mine to get the two-week rail pass.

This was my Interrail adventure, the quintessential backpackers' trip across Europe by train, though mine was without a backpack and done a bit too late to be called a rite of passage.

Some have referred to the Interrail pass as the modern version of the grand tour, that cultural and educational trip taken by young men, and the occasional young woman, from aristocratic or wealthy families in the seventeenth, eighteenth, and nineteenth centuries. The grand tour, usually undertaken at twenty-one and often with unlimited funds, could last anywhere from several weeks to several months, sometimes even years, and was expected to be the foundation of an aristocratic life. Later, aspiring bourgeoisie undertook the grand tour too. The route could vary but for the most part it took these privileged young people from the port of Dover in England to France and then on to Italy. The stops in between were determined by their own tastes and interests. They would hire what was referred to as a bear-leader, essentially a combination guardian and tutor, and take in the cultural monuments and museums, explore art galleries, and attend parties of the local elite. They would read books, listen to music, collect art, and sometimes commission original paintings, which they would bring home at the end of their stint. They were often known to carouse quite a bit.

Thus the Interrail pass could be seen as a more democratic version of the grand tour, and with the price of a pass at £27 when it first came into being in 1972, the equivalent of £308 today, its appeal was obvious, its popularity not surprising. If, during that time just before or after university I'd taken such a trip, the Interrail pass would have given me unlimited travel to twenty-one countries over the period of a month.

The pass started in celebration of the anniversary of the Union internationale des chemins de fer, which was created after World War II at a postwar peace conference at a time when the rise of nationalism, the confusion of railway lines that bisected borders, and a breakdown of trust meant that cross-continental trains were nearly at a standstill. The union was formed to provide standards and regulations, but mostly it was created to get Europe moving again.

What would it have meant to hear languages I could not identify, to see paintings I'd only known from the board game Masterpiece? I can now understand the urgency, the sense of being unencumbered I felt in this trip to France.

I can see the person I was then, happy to travel with a scant plan, with little money, and only rare calls home from a telephone booth. I was in a job I hated, and I was looking for more, but what that more might be was beyond me. Beyond my imagination that is, for I was a bit lost, drifting, denying that I was drawn to the arts, to reading, to writing. That I became determined to go to France, to travel by rail in a sort of free-spirited way that I would not have thought in my nature, was in hindsight a bursting through of my true self. Through whatever force, I decided I would go, and go alone if my friend couldn't afford it. I bought my rail pass, my flight ticket, prepared to travel on my own. Just a few weeks before I was to go, my friend said she could go after all so we looked at a map, drew an oval that started in Paris and went down the west side of France then over to Nice on the coast, then up the centre back to Paris, the points between to be determined.

⚜

In July of 1814, at the age of seventeen, Mary Shelley, then Mary Godwin, left England with Percy Bysshe Shelley, whom she would later marry, and her stepsister Claire Clairmont to go on a six-week tour of Europe. This trip would take them to France, Switzerland, Germany, and the Netherlands, and later Mary, with some input from Percy, would write about it in a travel book entitled *History of a Six Weeks' Tour*.

They arrive at Dover in a flurry, eager to make the crossing to France, for they were, in fact, running away, Mary having begun an affair with the married Percy. Rather than wait for the scheduled sailing the following day and perhaps be caught by Mary's father, they hire a sailor to take them across. It is the hottest day of the year, the air is still, the sky blue, and the sailor tells them it will take two hours. But at some point the weather turns, the wind picks up, the waves grow choppy, and Mary becomes dreadfully seasick. The seasickness, along with the stress of the wild ride, inexplicably causes her to fall asleep. The gale becomes more ferocious, the sailor admitting they are in a perilous situation, and still Mary sleeps, only to wake long enough to ask, How much longer?

They arrive at last in France, where the clouds have cleared, the sun ablaze, and Mary, walking into Calais, hears "for the first time the confused buzz of voices speaking a different language from that to which I had become accustomed." She observes the difference in dress to her native England, the hairstyles with high-piled coiffures, compares English maids to French ones, the latter less insolent than the former. Mary and her companions take a cabriolet to an inn, where later that day, Mary's stepmother will arrive in an attempt to convince her daughter, Claire, to return to England. The next day, despite persuasive arguments about her damaged reputation, Claire decides to remain with the couple and their adventure continues.

This to my mind, was Mary's version of the grand tour, though hers would be considered part of a new wave, that of Romantic travel, with a focus on spontaneity, with a view to acquiring experiences and good taste rather than objects. This new type of traveller would be open to new adventures, changing their itinerary frequently and travelling by any means they could find. Although few women took the grand tour, and those who did had a chaperone, I think Mary's version was always going to be different. She and her travelling companions had no such comforts as her male aristocratic predecessors on their grand tour. Although they followed a route that could be considered typical, they had little money and their trip seemed more akin to modern backpackers staying in cheap inns or hostels, their Interrail passes in hand. However, Mary did not have the benefit of trains, which were not yet in widespread use, instead travelling by foot, animal, cart, coach, and boat.

From the coast the trio goes to Paris, staying a week before deciding to walk through France, but Mary is not strong enough for such a journey so they buy an ass to carry their portmanteaus. The descriptions of this journey are vivid; her observations of the landscape and conditions of their accommodations paint a picture that is at times glorious, other times wretched. As I read her account, I think not so much of what she is seeing but rather how she is experiencing the trip. Two women, their long dresses dragging in the dirt, their male companion, perhaps with a walking stick. Were their shoes comfortable? What about food on those long stretches between villages? Did they pee along the side of the road?

They walk for hours, unsure when they would arrive at a village, or which village it might be. They sleep on straw with a thin mattress on top, rent a house with no furniture; they live on sour milk and stale bread, and it seems the first question when they enter a village, is whether they would be able to get good milk to drink. They begin worrying that their money will run out halfway through France and when Percy sprains his ankle he is forced to sit on the mule that replaced the ass, then in the cart hauled by the mule.

These hardships are twined around descriptions of the landscapes and observations of the people, one place so dirty and worn down by the recent Napoleonic Wars that some buildings had no roofs. They carry on to the next village, which is much cleaner and where the roofs have been rebuilt. Finally, in Switzerland they decide they must return to England. They have little money left and calculate that travelling the waterways will be cheaper, faster. They make their way back following inland rivers and canals, coming finally to another treacherous crossing of the English Channel.

When I first read of her account I thought it a rather reckless journey, planning from one day to the next, hiring animals as needed, in constant search for food that sometimes doesn't materialize. This doesn't match up with the elegant portraits I see of Mary—who would go on to write *Frankenstein*—that reveal a thoughtful, resting face usually in an elegant off-the-shoulder dress. I would have expected her journey to be like those of the aristocratic men who travelled that same route in great comfort. But I see now how thoroughly modern her trip was, how closely it mirrors in spirit the contemporary young person's impromptu lifestyle, their need to take risks, to explore places unknown. Looking back at my Interrail journey I could say the same—how reckless of me—but I was just doing as young people do, every day inventing a new plan.

I thought often of freedom during the lockdown, especially after reading of Mary Shelley's travels. Freedom to roam, to make last-minute plans to visit friends, to go out of my house and into my car and drive to Montreal, or Cleveland, or Detroit. The freedom to think about when things will change. That's what we lacked, the freedom to see the future. When Mary Shelley and her travelling companions ventured on their trip to Europe, it was the year after the end of the Napoleonic Wars that had seen conflict across Europe for more than a decade. The grand tour was halted during this period. No foreign travel was allowed. Could they have imagined a twelve-year moratorium on travel?

When we look back at the pandemic years, history will present it as a blip, one event in a long string of events across months and years. There is an elasticity to time, we learned. That March, the first month of lockdown, seemed to have three hundred days, and we drifted, as though through treacle, wondering, What next, what next?

Back in Blois after our day at the wineries, we realized I'd lost my passport. We'd cycled back to the town, where we'd booked a room in a pension that had French doors opening onto a river. We'd returned our bicycles, our muscles aching for a bath, our skin covered in sweaty dust, then after we'd got ready to go out to eat I noticed that the passport was gone.

J'ai perdu mon passeport, I told the policemen at the station, pleased I'd remembered the verb "lost" from my grade twelve French class.

We would take the train back to Paris the next day, I initially decided. We would find the Canadian embassy. We would have them send a replacement passport to . . . where? If we did not know where we were going, how would we know where to tell them to send it? We lobbed plans back and forth until we concluded that we really had to go to the police in Blois. I have no memory of any great concern or worry, just inconvenience. A day of our holiday lost. Perhaps it was that I had so much leeway on this journey, that we had a loose itinerary and the freedom of our rail pass that saved me from stress. Perhaps I was in denial.

After the police station, we wandered the streets, taking in a town with a population close to that of my hometown yet so vastly different in architecture, with its looming château, as to have landed me in a different era. This was long before smart phones, and I didn't have a camera so I have only my memory. The town was quiet after the frenetic pace of Paris, where we had taken in the likes of the Louvre, the Musée d'Orsay. My memory of Blois is this walk, the locals skittering across cobbled streets on their way home from work, the population sparse against the drama of the stone walls of the château. This I understood to be history, the living version of it, in which people could reside in buildings occupied for centuries, where signs of modernity were mere window-dressing. This was the beginning of my wish to live in such a place.

Finally, exhausted after our evening walk, we ate and returned to find a message from the innkeeper. It was from the police. My passport had been found on the lawn of the château where we'd lunched.

The next day we left Blois to spend a night in nearby Tours. From there we took the train to Bordeaux, where, stepping onto the platform, we quickly had a change of heart. The city was larger than expected, and we did not feel like navigating a busy urban centre. We jumped back on the train, taking our chances on St. Émilion, just down the line. These places had been random names on the map, not places we knew anything about, and with spontaneity as our guide we soon arrived at St. Émilion, its station at the edge of a field with the village a half-hour walk away. The village, we would discover, was known for its charm and wine, but our concern was bicycles and whether we could rent them.

The story of how we acquired bicycles is also the story of how we ended up staying overnight in the Montpellier train station, and involves a serendipitous meeting with an elderly man in the village centre. It could have been an entirely different story, especially as he took us back to his château, but it was one of kindness and generosity. We were eating an ice cream after having secured a place in a pension when he came up to us. My friend, as gregarious as I was reticent, took up the conversation and soon, in our poor French, we were asking where we might rent bicycles the next day. He could arrange it, he told us, and in appreciation, we invited him to join us for dinner. A few hours later he stood in front of our pension in his tweed jacket, clutching his hat to his chest. We went to the restaurant of a family he knew, they gathered at the table, nudging the young daughter to us so she might hear our English, perhaps say a word or two. We were something of a spectacle.

The next day he produced two white bicycles, like new, and we worried he'd misunderstood; we wanted to rent, not buy. But he had, in fact, rented them, and so we set off with food and map strapped to our bike to explore this area of French countryside. As we left, our self-appointed guide invited us to his château the next day, before we were to depart for Nice in the late afternoon.

The word "château" goes beyond the building and its architecture, and also becomes part of the name of the wine produced by its vineyard. In this case his estate was a modest affair. Still, after stopping by the house from which his elder brother, a man well past eighty, poked his head out in curiosity, our friend took us to where the wine was stored, a barn-like structure nearby. There, from the spigot of one of the four enormous vats, he poured us each a glass of wine. It was surreal. If we had been more sophisticated, if we had had more money, we would have bought a case, or ordered one to be sent home, but we were not and we had a train to catch, and of course he would take us to the station.

We had grown fond of our friend, and he of us. He knew the train to Nice and got us to the station in good time, and may have given us an instruction as we parted, our communication still rudimentary. I see him now, as we stood at the doors, him on the platform, again, his hat held to his chest, suddenly waving goodbye as the train pulled away.

We settled into the ten-hour journey, watching the vineyards and countryside that we'd just seen close up on our day of cycling pass by. We recounted our good luck, this strange encounter that had flavoured our time in St. Émilion, and began to think ahead to the beach in Nice. It was at Avignon that I realized we were off course. I knew the stations along the route, and knew that Avignon was not among them. I checked the map and saw that after coming from the west down to the coast we were now heading back up to the interior of France. I flagged the conductor, told him of our desire to go to Nice.

The train had separated two stations back he told us, we'd been in the wrong part of the train for Nice. The uncoupling our undoing. We would need to get off the train and take one to Montpellier to connect to Nice.

I remember that the Montpellier station was surprisingly busy for that time of night when we arrived, and outside in a large square people perambulated well past midnight. I remember trying to sleep in the plastic chairs while keeping an eye on our bags. I remember the young men from Turkey who kept trying to hit on us.

In the morning we caught the first train to Nice, found a small hotel, and went in search of the sea.

The final leg of our "grand tour" was the overnight train from Nice to Paris after a few days at the beach. This saved us the cost of a hotel and gave us an extra day in Nice. That extra day was spent in the sun and when we boarded our train, I could already see my skin turning red. We had booked a couchette, a room with six bunks, no privacy, just the ability to sleep in a horizontal position. I remember my skin on fire under a scratchy blanket. We slept with clothes on but the heat of my body meant I had to leave my legs uncovered. It is strange, this way of sleeping with strangers, and a hand reaching out to touch my leg should not have been a shock, but it was. A ghostly hand that I could not attribute to a particular body in our couchette.

What were his intentions, I wondered, pulling my leg away, to seduce me while the others slept?

❦

There is another layer to the story of Mary Shelley's grand tour. After I'd read *History of a Six Weeks' Tour* I came across a photo of an engraving of Villa Diodati, a mansion near Lake Geneva in Switzerland, with a caption revealing that Mary Shelley and her companions had stayed there visiting Lord Byron in summer 1816. She was travelling with Percy Bysshe Shelley and their four-month-old son, along with Claire Clairmont. She was still unmarried, but she referred to herself as Mrs. Shelley; she would not marry Percy until December of that year, shortly after his wife committed suicide. Mary's travel book is, in fact, an account of two journeys—the one in 1814 and another two years later in 1816. It is on this second trip where there are various accounts of them staying nearby and visiting Byron, or actually staying with him at the villa. Whatever the case, it was clear that they had spent at least some time there.

It is the second part of the book, in the form of letters, which describes this later journey. Here there is more of the weather, which was dreadful. In fact, 1816 was known as "the year without a summer." Global temperatures dropped significantly, in some cases causing food shortages, the abominable weather blamed on the volcanic eruption of Mount Tambora in Indonesia the year before. For Mary and the others, it meant spending long, gloomy hours at the villa, and one night with lightning flashing across Lake Geneva and the candles flickering in the villa, Lord Byron set the challenge for each of them to tell a gothic ghost story to pass the time. This was the genesis of *Frankenstein*, with Mary taking advantage of Byron's friend John Polidori's occupation as medical doctor to consult on questions of anatomy as she told her story. As for John Polidori's contribution to the challenge, he has been attributed as the author of "The Vampyre," believed to be the inspiration for Bram Stoker's *Dracula*, though there is some suggestion that Lord Byron might have had a hand in it.

After the Napoleonic Wars, the era of the grand tour faded away, with trains emerging later in the century as accessible transportation for all, a way of visiting places otherwise out of reach, both in Europe and in North America. Thomas Cook, from Derbyshire, England, was instrumental in setting up "tourism systems" such as organized tours—his first foray was to take a group of temperance campaigners by train to a rally eleven miles away. He was the first to organize trips abroad to the continent, beginning with a "grand circular tour" of Belgium, Germany, and France, and he introduced tickets that would be good for a certain set of days along pre-determined routes. He also introduced his own travel currency that lasted well into the twentieth century as travellers' cheques.

The organized tour has become a way of travelling that allows tourists access to places they would not go to on their own. This kind of trip is limited by the tour company's imagination and the traveller's budget, and while much may be gained, what is indubitably lost is individuality, spontaneity, and the art of discovery. Stefan Zweig, a committed train traveller who travelled and wrote across Europe and published *Journeys*, a collection of essays on his travels before World War II, was fearful of the "bureaucratic, automated" industry of mass tourism then in its infancy. He believed in the need for individuality, for travel to be representative of one's own taste, one's own needs—a belief I have come to share.

~~~

The resurgence of the modern-day grand tour through Interrail steadily grew from its inception in 1972 until it peaked in the early 1990s. In 1998 it offered passes to adults. It was the deregulation of airlines that saw its decline, when cheap flights meant train travel became unfashionable. But this is changing again, with the environmental impact of air travel a significant factor in the recent jump in Interrail passes to the thirty-three countries in the network. According to the *Financial Times*, the "flight shame" movement that started in Sweden in 2018 is reported to have helped Interrail sales rise there by 40 percent from 2017 to 2018, and by 2019, across Europe sales rose to 300,000, again with the majority of buyers stating concern about their carbon footprint as the reason for travelling by train. Sales have recently returned to these pre-pandemic levels.

It has been many years since that two-week journey through France that would change my world view. It would set my sights on Europe as a place I wanted to live. Perhaps it is not yet too late for me to go Interrailing again, perhaps I could see things anew even after all these years. It may be the moment for it, this time following Mary Shelley's route, maybe with a backpack.

Escape: *The* Train Compartment

Only travellers in the first and second classes
enjoyed the shelter of closed and roofed cars.
The others sat on crowded benches with the wind
roaring over them so that they were unable to talk,
the smoke stinging their eyes and nostrils; when it
rained they had to open up their umbrellas.

—Wolfgang Schivelbusch, *The Railway Journey:*
The Industrialization of Time and Space
in the Nineteenth Century

It was on a Saturday night, just after ten p.m. on July 9, 1864, that two bank clerks entered a carriage on a train in Hackney Station, London, and saw blood all over the cushions. The guard, who was quickly alerted, found a black beaver hat, a stick, and a bag in the compartment, but no body. He contacted the authorities, who ordered the train taken to the next station to be detached for inspection. Later that night, a train travelling in the opposite direction came upon a severely injured man by the side of the road, later identified as Thomas Briggs, seventy years old, chief clerk at a bank. Briggs later died of his injuries. The stick and bag were confirmed to be his but not the hat. Robbery was believed to be the motive as his watch, chain, and gold eyeglasses were missing.

This was a murder that gripped Victorian England, a shocking case for the media at the time and more recently the subject of the book *Mr Briggs' Hat: A Sensational Account of Britain's First Railway Murder* by Kate Colquhoun, as well as a documentary, *Murder on the Victorian Railway*. The murder became headline news because of its gruesome nature and the fact that it was a "gentleman" who'd been killed, but most significantly because it was the first murder to be carried out on a train in Britain. People were already suspicious of this fast form of transportation; for many, the murder was the last straw.

Compartments within carriages at that time were self-contained with no way to travel or communicate between them, the only access directly to a station platform. Each one was essentially a locked room. This heightened the sense of danger and the newspapers made much of it. The *London Review* reported, "Worst of all is the horrid consciousness not merely that you are uneasy, but that you are making the travellers in the opposite corner uneasy too . . . you know as the train rolls on that though he may pretend to be looking out the window, your vis-à-vis is keeping half an eye on your movements, just as you are keeping half an eye on his."

Because of the high-profile case, the authorities appointed Richard Tanner to investigate, a man recognized for his brilliance in detective work. At the time, fingerprint identity or blood tests were still in the future, and indeed even the notion of a detective was a relatively new concept. All Tanner had to work with was the physical evidence of the mysterious hat, and a ring and watch chain later found in the carriage. A hefty reward of £300 was offered and 2,000 posters were pasted all over London. Thousands of letters poured in, among them a promising clue from a jeweller, the wonderfully named John Death, who said the gold chain had been brought in for exchange by a man with a German accent, who bought a cheaper one along with a ring. The next clue came from a cab driver who said he knew a man who owned a beaver hat similar to the one from the carriage—a young German tailor named Franz Müller.

Tanner tracked down Müller's address, but he was too late. Müller had left three days before on the sailing ship *Victoria* bound for the United States. Thus began the chase. Tanner requested permission to go after Müller and, along with another officer, he took Death, the jeweller, and Matthews, the cab driver, with him on the night express train to Liverpool to board the steamship *City of Manchester*.

The newspapers were close on the heels of this transatlantic hunt that had captured the public's imagination, even knocking news of the American Civil War off the front page. Steamships were faster than sailing ships but still the journey took two and a half weeks. When they entered New York Harbour they would have to wait a further three weeks before the *Victoria* arrived.

It's at this point in the story that I have to pause and consider the details. I'm trying to imagine these two officers travelling with the two witnesses. What would they talk about on the train on that first leg of their pursuit? The case? Or would that seem unprofessional? Perhaps they didn't talk at all, instead leaning into the headrests in their compartment to get some sleep before boarding the ship. And what of the two-and-a-half-week voyage, how would they occupy their time then? Would the detectives press the cab driver for more details, would they ask the jeweller for a better description? Would they all dine together, spend the evening playing cards? It's inconceivable now in our world of instant results to think of participants in a crime case taking five weeks out of their lives to travel in order to capture and return a criminal. Then, of course, there was the three-week wait for the sailing ship with the suspect on board. What it must have been like for the cab driver, even the jeweller, to be dropped into this adventure that would take them to New York. Presumably they would not have known travel like this, exploring a new city, treated as expert witnesses. Perhaps they were put up in a hotel, fêted.

Through our modern lens this would be considered slow travel, and therefore a lesson in patience. But to be at sea for weeks was the norm at the time. Such voyages held their own suspension of time and loose adherence to a schedule. The fact that this was a thrilling crime adventure conjures up swift and decisive movements. We might project a pace expected in today's world with people dashing about, giving urgent orders. But because they didn't know any other way, they would have had to accept the leisurely days at sea, sipping tea, reading a book, conversing with fellow passengers. They would not be at the bow of the ship madly searching for land, with one eye on their watch.

꙳

When the *Victoria* finally docked, Tanner boarded the ship and arrested Müller, who denied the charge. After an extradition process the party returned to England. Müller was tried and, despite his insistent plea of innocence, was pronounced guilty and sentenced to hang. Forty thousand people, many drunk and rowdy, gathered in the narrow streets near the Old Bailey for the execution. This would be the last public hanging in England. Müller's last words? "I did it."

This case followed another sensational murder that had taken place in France four years prior: a Mr. Poinsot, one of the presidents of the law courts, was killed while travelling first class, his throat slit. "He was quite dead," reported the *Richmond Times-Dispatch*. The unknown murderer, who had got out the instant the train stopped and was never caught, disappeared. He had robbed his victim of everything valuable.

These two murders were significant as they would lead to the development of the corridor that runs along compartments. Robbery and assault on women were already widespread, but murder meant something really had to be done to provide safe travel in these "locked boxes." Initial ideas ranged from having a speaker tube that ran the length of the train, to a cord that could activate an alarm, to an arrangement of mirrors that would enable train personnel to see into the compartments. The solution adopted on some trains was a peephole between compartments, which became known as Müller's Lights, after the famed murderer.

It was becoming obvious that passengers should be able to travel freely through the train. The first solution was to put a door in the compartments so that they would open on to the next, but this soon bolstered the argument against the North American open-carriage system, since privacy was compromised with other passengers traipsing through compartments, and the noise too disruptive. A study by Ernest Dapples in 1866, commissioned by French and English train rail companies that took into account the psychology of European travellers, revealed that "the passengers would complain if they were obliged to spend a long time in public carriages, subjected to all the noises, vulnerable to all eyes and all ears."

Eventually, a corridor was introduced with sliding doors to separate the passengers from the traffic between cars, and the peace and isolation, not to mention the class distinction, so desired by European travellers, was maintained.

※

The corridor was not a place of escape that one summer when, in my early thirties, I sat in a compartment, my then partner and I lucky to find seats on the train from Warsaw to Sopot, the seaside town next to Gdańsk, known as Poland's Riviera. Sopot would be my home for the next year. It was by the sea, had the longest pier in Europe, a posh Grand Hotel on its shore, and an annual televised pop concert at the Forest Opera bandshell—it seemed an idyll.

The Berlin Wall was not long down and Poland was opening up, but the mark of Communism was still evident. There were few cars on the road, and the nationalized trains were cheap and crowded. Eventually, I learned to buy first-class tickets there; they were inexpensive, less crowded, and safer.

But on that day, the parched, wide-open landscape of the Polish farmland outside my window was a dizzying contrast to the atmosphere on the train: the corridor jammed, people sitting on suitcases, standing with books in hand, talking to friends. We were on the other side of the glass, trapped like zoo animals, six of us in the stifling compartment. The mood was subdued, the space filled with suitcases, large plastic checkered bags—a ubiquitous Eastern European carry-all. We were getting used to each other's presence. No one was going anywhere.

I watched the man across from me in the middle seat pull out a lunch to share with his wife: kielbasa, bread, cheese, pickles. We glanced, then turned away as he spread the paper that held the bread across his knee and placed the food out as if on a tray. It was hard not to be part of this picnic because of proximity, the smell of kielbasa present to all of us. In my time living in Poland, I would come to recognize this lack of inhibition in those occupying public space. Hours spent in queues over the years had conditioned them well.

The shouting broke the mood, jolted us from our introspection. I looked up at the woman who sat directly across from me, wondering what had upset her so, and glanced at my partner for help. Who was she yelling at? What was the problem? Then I realized . . . her eyes stared straight ahead. It was me she was yelling at. My heart raced, a sudden sickening feeling took over. People on the other side of the glass were looking at her now, and at me. Back and forth. What's happening? I whispered to my partner, fluent in Polish, who remained mute. His silence against her onslaught startled me and foreshadowed so much behaviour that would eventually be the undoing of this relationship.

Your seat, he said finally.

But she has one?

He shrugged.

Slowly, eventually, the shouting subsided, like a toy whose battery has run out. Then silence.

She just wanted to blow off steam, my partner told me when we arrived at the flat where we would live that year.

But steam from what, I wanted to know. The poverty, the years of Communism, the rising price of food, the lack of jobs—these things I would understand later. I would also come to admire the fiery spirit that gave Poles resilience as well as a great capacity to complain if things were not going well. I would learn how hard it was for them to accept that foreigners like me were moving in, a sure sign of disruption. The Wall had come down and the world rejoiced. Except for those who didn't, those who had lived on a fixed income and knew only of cheap goods, how to navigate half-filled shelves, how to barter for services, for that last pair of size thirty-nine shoes on the shelf. *I can fix your plumbing if you sell them to me.* Change is hard, sometimes life altering.

We moved to this beautiful town by the sea, I set up a school with individual lessons for twenty students desperate to learn English, and we walked the beach just a block from our home, but the energy that had kept us together for two years and made sense of a move to his native Poland, would become dangerously charged. Like those train passengers in that locked box, I would need an escape.

⁂

The photos of Sopot I see now on travel sites bear little resemblance to the town I lived in, which had few cafés, no beach bars, and one local cinema run by two elderly women—one would sell you a ticket, the other would collect it ten feet away by the curtain that led to the cinema. "Smooth Operator" by

Sade would invariably be playing while we waited for the film to start and when the film ended one of the elderly women would switch on the glaring overhead lights the minute the credits began, startling the audience. The other was stationed at the side door with her jacket on, waiting for you to leave. Once while watching a film, a cat walked across the back of the chairs two rows ahead of us.

Sopot had gone from fishing village to spa town when one of Napoleon's physicians, Jean Georg Haffner, discovered the healing power of the saline waters in 1823 and built a bathing house and the famous pier. There is a rich history of diplomats, aristocrats, and the wealthy from across the country coming to this town, first for the spa, then to lose their fortunes at the beachside Kasino Hotel, now known as the Grand Hotel.

The remnants of Communism were everywhere when I lived there, and despite its rich history and location, the town seemed worn, tired, unaffected by the "progress" being made in other parts of the country.

Don't go to a café on your own, my partner warned. They will think you're a prostitute.

And so I roamed the streets, daring to go into shops and request items from behind the counter in my rudimentary Polish. It was through these wanderings that I discovered the train that would take me to the city of Gdynia on one side of Sopot, or Gdańsk on the other.

Gdynia, a modern shopping town, held little interest except for my curiosity about the lure of capitalism for Poles. (I discovered that Levi's sold for a hundred American dollars, half the average monthly salary then.) But it was Gdańsk that I returned to most often. Its medieval architecture surrounded the marketplace, where sellers sold goods from bras to handmade amber jewellery laid out on blankets or little folding tables.

The looming cranes beyond the old town were a constant reminder that history was made in this town by Lech Wałęsa, the former shipyard electrician turned activist, who roused workers as leader of Solidarity, a Polish trade union and pro-democratic force. It was this movement that ushered in the end of Communist rule in Poland and would eventually contribute to the fall of the Berlin Wall.

My English lessons were mostly an exercise in conversation, and I spent hours offering prompts and asking students questions: How did you shop when shelves were empty? Tell me about the bartering system. What did you do during the holidays? Describe Christmas Day. And because the docks were so much part of this community, a question to a merchant seaman who was so keen to learn: Tell me about the workings of a sextant.

Back and forth I went on this train that allowed me to wander on my own, to explore the area, to be both tourist and resident. The area was opening up to Western ways, but there was an atmosphere of hidden danger. Along with the tip to avoid cafés on my own, I was warned that taxi drivers were often part of a local mafia and would charge exorbitant rates, or worse. There may have been truth in this but I had the sense that paranoia lingered, a leftover of Communist rule.

On an early trip to Gdańsk, pleased with my new independence, I settled into a seat and showed the inspector my ticket when he came through, but this did not satisfy him. He stood in the crowded carriage, hovering over me, berating me in Polish. My eyes pleaded to my neighbours for help, and finally a young woman told me that I should have stamped the ticket when boarding the train.

Later I would wonder if perhaps I should have taken these incidents of Poles admonishing me as a warning—*Leave, now,* they might have been saying, *this situation is not good for you.* As my relationship eroded I spent more time on this train, my getaway. I was going deeper in the Polish culture—more questions asked of my students, language skills building so I could buy carrots and tomatoes from the local market, order a taxi, or have a rudimentary conversation. I was sometimes invited to dinner by students' families and once I took the train to Kraków with the daughter of one, a businessman who imported televisions from Korea.

The train was my liberation.

I did eventually go to the café at the Grand Hotel for a coffee and cake, perhaps my own small act of protest. I was too curious, and frankly didn't care if they thought I was a prostitute.

❦

By then, I knew it was time to leave, but my decampment would not be easy. My relationship was over but I had become infatuated with Poland.

A frank conversation with Grazyna, a student who, with her husband, ran a local bakery and whose daughter I also taught, turned into a series of fortunate events. She arranged a meeting in her living room with the undersecretary of foreign affairs in the Polish government, a friend. They were looking for people to work at a foreign investor agency in Warsaw, he told me; he would arrange an interview.

The details of this journey, clandestine, explained as a shopping trip with Grazyna, I barely remember. But the feeling of escape, of overwhelming relief the trip offered as I boarded the train, of a future unencumbered, was like a full-body sigh I'd been waiting for. That, I do recall.

The interview at the agency in an historic building across from the British embassy took place in what could be described as a small ballroom. I knew little about the job other than it would be in the communications department, and I was nervous with Klaus, the German consultant, and Elisabeth, the British one who interviewed me, but I could sense that the new beginning I needed was within reach.

A week later I would get the job offer, and two weeks after that I would board the last train I would take from Sopot.

꩜

I did not suffer a crime on the trains in Poland, though one night on the way home from work in Warsaw I did get mugged in an underground pedestrian walkway. Two young men jumped from nowhere, one grabbing my satchel that I held onto until my stupid and relentless screaming finally wore them down and they ran off. The trains had given me the independence I needed while living in this country, but the mugging was a message that I had to be forever watchful.

Women
and Travel

*I won't travel alone with a woman—I promise
you that.*

—Wilkie Collins, *The Letters of Wilkie Collins,*
Volume 1

In the summer of 2001, trains approaching Norwich, England, drove through swarms of Painted Lady butterflies attracted by the great swathes of Buddleia bushes growing by the tracks. This bush with purple, coned-shaped inflorescences is not native to the region, but was introduced to the UK from China in the 1890s. Its seeds were carried up and down the country in trains' wakes, and now it's hard to imagine going for a walk without seeing the droopy-headed bushes. The Oxford ragwort was also spread in this manner, originating from the Oxford Botanic Gardens, whose botanists had procured it from its native Sicily. Its seeds were picked up by the rush of wind from trains and it, too, is now ubiquitous. The botanist George Claridge Druce caught the process in action, having seen a seed from the plant drift into his train carriage in Oxford, then float in the air until it blew out twenty miles down the road in Tilehurst, Berkshire.

❧

The idea of trains having an influence on what is grown along the tracks was the subject of a recent study in France undertaken by the National Museum of Natural History. Migration and connectivity are usually associated with the movement of people on trains, but this study examined plants that appeared along the edges of rail tracks. Focussing on two specific tracks that ran through densely populated areas south of Paris, researchers first assessed the unique characteristics of each track's plant community. Their hypothesis was that if trains increased plant connectivity, those that grew along each track should be similar. They discovered that floral plants did indeed have similarity along each track line, rather than between the two separate tracks, indicating that trains were dispersing the seeds along their route. The presence of train stations didn't interfere with the migration of seeds but overpasses did break the chain to some degree. This has led to discussion of the design of overpasses, and whether they should be wider and deliberately planted in order to improve the connectivity even further.

❧

That image of the seed swirling and dancing through the air as it moved forward along the train stays with me as I think of the day, just two years after the Painted Lady invasion, that I left Norwich station, on my way to Bangor, Wales, a journey that took me from one of the farthest points east to one of the farthest west in Great Britain.

I've left Norwich by train many times over the years but was unaware that it used to have three train stations, one of which was damaged in April 1942 in the Baedeker Raids. Norwich, York, Bath, Canterbury, and Exeter were chosen as targets because of their cultural significance. Baedeker was the title of the German tourist guidebook that marked out places of cultural and archeological importance, and the raids were done in retaliation to attacks on German targets by the Royal Air Force. Norwich had been my home for eight years, and though this leaving was temporary, soon it would be permanent. On this trip I was five months pregnant, heading to a writing retreat near the Irish Sea in Wales.

～❦～

"Thou shalt not be overcome." These, the words of Julian of Norwich, a fourteenth-century anchoress—one who becomes walled into a church room for a life of prayer and contemplation—and mystic who lived in a cell in the church for which she was named, just a few minutes' walk from my work. This is not the most quoted passage from her book, *Revelations of Divine Love*, the first to be written in English by a known female writer, but it is one I prefer. One might find the simplicity of it soothing, like a mantra in times of war and plague.

Julian lived through the Black Death, when at least a third of the population of Norwich died, including her husband and child. She became ill herself, was thought to be dying and was even given the last rites after she lost her eyesight and her body became numb. She then had a series of visions, or "shewings," of

Jesus. She recovered from the illness, became an anchoress and spent the rest of her life in the small cell in St. Julian's Church on King Street, receiving visitors and food from a small window, but otherwise left alone with her thoughts and her writing. She is remembered as much for her life as an anchoress as for her writing. When the plague returned, she may have been saved by her life in quarantine.

Because I have been to the cell where she lived, having worked nearby, it is her chosen way of living more than her theology I have thought about over the years and think about now when looking back at my own period of isolation during lockdown. Julian's cell is a stark but bright room, and it existed in the middle of a town that was bustling with commerce in her time, a constant rabble of people just steps from her window. I think about how she cultivated solitude that would have allowed her to be separate rather than isolated. Solitude would have given her the time to consider her faith deeply, as she desired, but I expect there would have been a reckoning with herself as well, the things that might have made her fearful or content. There would be a sense of protection in this space, valuable only if one was at ease with one's own existence.

In our period of being moored to our homes, forced upon us for our protection, we had our own reckoning. Some faced sickness, death, and financial hardship, while some thrived, taking up exercise, bird-watching, bread baking. For many, it was fear, loneliness, an inner chaos not so easily explained that marked our lives. Perhaps for Julian, sitting in her cell looking out into the world through her window, it would be the first time she would fully encounter herself. The same might be said of my own experience, where from my "cell" I came to realize aspects of myself that had not been tested before, especially in dealing with the constant anxiety over illness.

The reality of her isolation, however, was extreme. She had chosen to be an anchoress and would have known what it entailed, but when I read that she was actually sealed in this cell, not able to leave, I found it hard to imagine the level of faith it would have taken to make such a decision. It also puts in perspective the mad desire many of us had to leave our homes during our own period of quarantine, comparatively brief in hindsight. That she lived in her cell for at least twenty years, aside from igniting the claustrophobic in me, speaks to a patient adherence to her beliefs, and the ability to cope with doubts—and it's terrifying to learn that she had at times regretted her decision to live such an isolated life. Somehow it underscores that word—"resilience"—bandied around during our own experience of a pandemic. This trait apparently as old as all humanity.

I didn't see swarming butterflies nor drifting seeds when my train departed Norwich. My mind was too occupied with what was ahead. Once I boarded the train, I was free to leave the details of our forthcoming international move behind. I could forget about my job and about packing, and appointments with the midwife. For the next week my identity would be that of a writer and so I settled in, sitting upright in the rigid seats, observant of fellow travellers. Had I remembered to bring my notes?

The train eased out of the station and I waved goodbye, mirroring any number of film scenes where from the window one bids farewell to one's loved one. The goodbyes on trains are often tinged with melancholy or regret—arms reaching out for that last touch. But we felt more stunned than anything after breathless months of planning our leave-taking, heads bowed over countless forms and decisions, the thought of saying goodbye for a week left us both feeling as though we were roaming wild. Nothing was ordinary back then, and the fact of my long-awaited pregnancy weighed heavily on both of us. Was I wise to travel when everything felt so fragile?

But the train soothes, and soon I was looking forward to my destination, past Cambridge, through the Midlands, and finally into Wales. I was skip-hopping across the web of railway routes, changing trains in Stockport, Crewe, and Chester. I knew little of where I would spend the week, only that there would be sixteen of us, plus two tutors, and our base for the week would be Tŷ Newydd, the summer home of the former prime minister David Lloyd George.

Lloyd George, known for his skill in seeing Great Britain out of the Great War, for granting partial suffrage to women, and for laying the foundation for a welfare state, died in the library of his beloved Tŷ Newydd. Although he supported suffragists—not the militant variety of activists—and progress was made for women under his leadership, it was not without incident.

When invited to open the village hall in nearby Llanystumdwy, Lloyd George was silenced by shouts of "Votes for Women." The incident almost got out of control when one of the women was nearly thrown over the bridge into the River Dwyfor. Lloyd George was still chancellor of the exchequer when his house, under construction in Surrey, was bombed by Emmeline Pankhurst in protest of his lack of support for the cause. She was found guilty and sentenced to three years at

Holloway Prison, where she began a hunger strike. Pankhurst was never force-fed—it was considered too controversial to inflict this practice on such a high-profile activist—and soon after, legislation known as the Cat and Mouse Act was passed that allowed temporary release so a prisoner's health could improve before returning to complete their sentence.

But I would only learn about these connections to Tŷ Newydd later, just as I learned that there were rumours about the library at the house being haunted by a young boy who wanders there at night, sometimes moving books around.

For the moment I settled into my seat, drew out my notebook, ordered a decaffeinated coffee from the drinks trolley, and watched the fields of Norfolk pass by.

In writing about Lloyd George and suffragettes, and the writers I would spend the week with at Tŷ Newydd, I became distracted by crinolines. Perhaps, because it turned out that all the writing retreat participants were women—an unusual makeup according to organizers—and the fact that my body was just beginning to change at the time, I remember this trip as one particularly devoted to women and women's concerns. It has caused me to think of women and travel, particularly how they travelled in other periods. This is where crinolines come in. In the index of the book on trains I've been reading, the section on "women" includes categories such as station lavatories, waiting rooms, and refreshment room staff, but my attention is caught by the entries assaults on, blackmail by, prostitution, and crinolines.

I try to picture myself with my suitcase and bag of note-books negotiating the aisles of the train and squeezing into a compartment wearing a whalebone corset and yards of fabric. My body seemed to be carrying its own excess bag-gage, so could I imagine the burden of my dress if travelling at the height of "crinolinemania," when entire factories were devoted to producing the steel hoops and stores ded-icated to the sale of crinolines. The steel-hooped crinolines were known as a cage crinoline, and there is something of this—the sense of being trapped—that the women must have surely felt but considered worth it for the sake of fashion. The fact that there was danger in wearing these crinolines, with dresses catching fire, or getting caught in machinery or car-riage wheels, makes it impossible for most modern women to understand the appeal.

Yet appeal it did. Crinolines could reach a diameter of six feet, and in 1850 when the steel hoops replaced other mate-rials such as whalebone and cane, it was seen as a revolution in design. The *Lady's Newspaper* in 1863 described it thus: "So perfect are the wave-like bands that a lady may ascend a steep stair, lean against a table, throw herself into a carriage without inconveniencing herself or others . . . and lastly, it allows the dress to fall in graceful folds." The steel hoops had the advan-tage over previous versions of being lightweight but somewhat flexible when moving through doorways or in such places as a railway carriage. It was clear that there was no escaping the crinoline if you were a woman travelling in this period, and it's hard to imagine the impact that it had in a train compartment at a time when clergy were protesting that crinolines reduced capacity in churches by a third.

The crinoline also makes an appearance in stories of blackmail by women living on the fringes of the law who took advantage of men in the isolation of the compartment by initiating an assault. They banked on a man's desire to remain silent about the incident and offer payment due to the public humiliation he would endure if word got out. In one case, a Reverend George Capel was accused of putting his hands between a young servant's legs as she walked past him in the compartment, after which she turned and called him a "nasty beast." Witnesses of both sexes, as well as the accused, claimed the contact was inadvertent as he was trying to push her crinoline away from him as she went past. When the details of the case were printed in the press, it was the phrase "nasty beast" that brought forth a witness who'd had a similar experience: a young woman had thrown her crinoline across his knees, then accused the man of assault with those same damning words. The irony of these offences is that assaults on women were far more common at the time, the isolation of the compartment a waiting crime scene. But these stories where men were the apparent victims, were taken very seriously, prompting a magistrate in one case to state that there were "many young and inexperienced men travelling by rail, totally unprotected" and he called on railway companies to designate men-only carriages. They also made men, such as the writer Wilkie Collins, wary about travelling alone with a woman in a compartment.

The vulnerability of women travelling alone is evidenced in the case of eighteen-year-old Mary Ann Moody in 1864. She was followed into a carriage by a middle-aged man named Henry Nash, who pestered her with questions and unwanted offers of help with her luggage. Despite her attempts to ignore him, he persisted, eventually reaching a hand out to touch her shoulder, then slid it down to her waist and further until he began to lift her dress. Looking to escape, she took the only option available. At Nash's hearing, she told the court that she understood the dangers of climbing out from a moving train and the possible fine it might entail but "my character, my welfare, everything that is worth having in this world, is far dearer to me than my life, and therefore I jumped out of the carriage."

And here is where I return to the matter of fashion, wondering whether she would have been wearing a crinoline, which had started to wane in popularity by 1860, or the less restrictive slimline dress with a bustle that was becoming the style. This is important as I'm picturing a crinoline flapping in the rushing wind while a bustle might have been easier to control as she clutched to the side of the moving train. In either case the situation would have been harrowing as she crept along, reaching for her rescuer, a man named Stokes who managed to grab her from his window in the next carriage just as she fainted. He held her for a further five miles until labourers were able to signal to the driver to stop the train.

꧁꧂

There were no "nasty beasts" or groping pests on my train, but late in the day on the Chester leg, two young men burst into the carriage, each wielding a tall can of beer, their loud and self-important voices threatening to me. Though the carriage was larger and more open than a compartment, I was uneasy their drunken burst would take a turn, and I noticed that everyone held their heads bent over a book, or fixed on the outside view, anything to avoid eye contact.

The rail map of England looks like it was planned on an Etch A Sketch, main lines with branch lines that reach out to various end points drawn as straight lines and sharp corners so it looks as though most of the country is not far from one of the 2,563 stations. The station stops on this nine-hour journey gave me the chance to get out and walk around and escape my unsavoury fellow travellers. Because the closer we got to Bangor, the more sparsely populated the carriage, I became more aware of my fellow travellers, as if we were together on this expedition to North Wales.

At some point I stopped looking back in my thoughts and started looking ahead. I peered out the window, wanting to imprint every possible thing on my memory. This is what happens when I travel, the lingering stress of getting ready and departing finally gives way to what lies ahead.

As the carriage thinned out with every stop, I began to think about what this week alone with my writing might do for me. This inflection point on my trips comes as a surprise to me, always. What have I been waiting for? Why am I stuck in the worries of my everyday life? This time is mine to enjoy. And so there I was, finally eager, looking at the indifferent Welsh countryside, feeling myself open to the mounting excitement of what was coming.

As I was held at home by the pandemic, I turned to films and books for the pleasure of new places. I watched *Summertime*, a David Lean film starring Katharine Hepburn, and was reminded of the fervour that travel can elicit. The film is the story of Jane Hudson, a middle-aged woman travelling to Venice on her own. The opening scene is of the train shooting along the water just minutes from the entrance of the city (just as I would shoot past the Irish Sea at the entrance to Bangor at the end of my journey). Soon we're inside the compartment, where Jane, standing with camera in hand, is holding out a brochure to a man reading a paper. Hold it up, she instructs him. She takes a photo, as if this will be the title page of her holiday photo album.

The gentleman asks if she's been to Venice before. No, she tells him, have you? He's been several times, he tells her. Several times! She can hardly believe it, pauses in her picture-taking. I hope you are going to like it, he says to her. She looks at him, suddenly fretful. Like it? As if there was any other possibility. Like it, she says to him, the waters of Venice glistening in the background through the train window. I've got to. I've come such a long way. I've saved such a long time for this trip. Do you think, maybe, I won't like it? She is crestfallen, her enthusiasm drained away for just that moment. The possibility that, after all that anticipation, the expectation, the planning, she won't like Venice. The man reassures her and he is so charming and handsome that I expected this to be the romantic turn in the story. But no, it swerves away from him once we establish that he is the veteran traveller, she the wide-eyed novice, and the zeal we see from her is for the city itself, the journey she is on. And so we see a woman, travelling independently, taking photographs in a way that is artful, thoughtful.

People travel more readily now, with cheap flights and tourism packaged in so many ways from bachelor weekends to wellness retreats. In 1950 there were 25 million international tourists, and by 2019 that had grown to 1.5 billion. Economic prosperity, improvements in transportation, and increased leisure time all contribute to this surge. There is an expectation of travel not possible a generation ago. At the time this film was made, in the mid-fifties, the trip Jane took would have been a once-in-a-lifetime adventure.

We do, I know, interpret films from our own distinct vantage point, our own preferences, but I am moved by her energy and think about how blasé we've become to the experience of travel, how we no longer let ourselves be taken over by it.

There is a subplot to the movie where Jane meets an American couple on their retirement trip. They have a full itinerary planned by someone back in their hometown, things they need to see, a schedule that must be adhered to, until they are given their two hours of free time. There is a marked contrast between their travels and Jane's experience. Some travellers journey to conquer, others to savour.

The passion Jane feels for the city reminded me of the spell that can be cast by a place. And though I did not know it yet as I sat on that train to Bangor, I felt it, a kind of overtaking that would make this journey significant. So when the pandemic made travel out of the question, the film became an aide-mémoire of a spell previously cast, a yearning or desire that comes from being in a place altogether different from the familiar.

What I know about train travel is that it gives me a much needed sense of propulsion while allowing me to be still. That is at the heart of it, I think, that I am getting somewhere, even if it turns out the most significant journey is the internal one.

We cannot know the internal journey that Jane takes, but there are clues. She checks into her hotel, ventures out sightseeing, stops at a café, a restaurant, and throughout there is a humming excitement. But there is also a trace of uncertainty.

Should she be alone in the café, would it be better to have a dinner companion? These are words not spoken, but we see the hesitation, the glances to others who have arrived in pairs. Given that this movie was released in 1955, this character seems out of step with the era, those postwar years that sent women back to the home to cook and procreate after stepping up so ably while the men were at war. Independence was over. A woman's place was in her home. Having lived in a country where I ran the risk of being branded a prostitute for sitting alone in a café, I had an inkling of what it meant for her to be alone like that, the sense of being marked as someone odd and out of place. To be unseen amidst a crowd.

But perhaps I am making too much of this. The movie is a romance, after all. A man does enter the picture eventually, love ensues, complicated love, but I see the passion for him intertwined with that of the place, her own sense of being, brimming with life in this city, because that is what can happen when you embark on a journey. You find you are closer to yourself than you have ever been.

The point at which I was able to give myself over to this retreat started on the train but there was so much more that would make it special. The house for one, slightly worn, with an elegance that comes from all the people who have lived there. The whitewashed exterior, bay windows that overlooked fields where cows roamed, the Irish Sea in the distance. One night after each of us had read our work in the library with the bay window that looked out to fields and sea, I called my husband as I walked through the dewy grass of the lawn and told him how happy I was to be there, teasing that I didn't want to leave. We had all entered a state of bliss, cast-offs who had lost inhibitions. We were writing and making friends in this splendid isolation.

But before that, I sat in the last leg of the train from Chester to Wales with my suitcase at my feet. The thing about train travel is that it is largely a pastoral view once clear of the urban areas where the stations are, and this can be nothing but restful. I must have known that this is what I needed when so much of my life was about to change.

❧

It was Penelope I befriended most at Tŷ Newydd. We talked between sessions, dodged cows in the fields as we walked towards the sea. We talked about our writing, confided things not usually revealed to strangers. As can happen with travel friendships, we fell out of touch, but then found each other in recent years through social media, where we continue to track each other's lives. We are still occasionally in touch. I sometimes place too much weight on these situational friendships, but it can feel like being rescued in some way, to have a connection, even if fleeting, that buoys you, and gives the experience of being there more meaning.

At night we took turns cooking before gathering around the large square table in the kitchen. On my night to cook I was peeling carrots with one of the women, a biochemist who, outside the retreat, was in the same writing group as Mary Lawson, whose book *Crow Lake* had just been published. She talked about how excited they were when her book was published, the breakthrough writer in the group. I asked her about her work as a biochemist, and she talked about charred food, how carcinogenic it was, and since then I have not been able to look at blackened food on a barbecue without thinking of that conversation. The British writer Michèle Roberts was our tutor, vibrant and always encouraging. She would sit with us at night after the readings, drink wine, and be part of the group.

On the last night, after the final reading, after much wine had been drunk, there was a great sense of merriment in the group and we drifted out to the expansive lawn. Under a bright moon everyone started running and dancing about. A kind of unbridled joy that could only happen because we were so far away from everything, had spent the week escaping our old lives, and felt a rare moment of childish freedom. I was not drinking wine and was not up to running about but I was with them out there, floating around in the garden, soaking up the damp night air tinged with the smell of sea and cow dung.

Memories can be underrated but that was largely what we had under lockdown. The lived experience of going away, of travelling, was not possible, but this time offered a rare period of extended reflection, not just of where I had been but how each trip had shaped me. This was not a mourning for glory days, rather these recollections were like the stray marble found in a box of papers, a note received from an old friend, the shaky handwriting of a grandmother's letter. None of them amounted to much on their own, so I dismissed them. But they accumulate, and gain strength. If we remember the smell of leather from a childhood car, if we remember the thrill of our first hotel pool, if we remember the sound of a mournful train whistle from a Midwestern town, we remember who we were in that moment.

⁕

In the end Jane must leave, both the city and her lover. She leans out the train window, looking for him. But it is Venice she is leaving as well, her memories, a version of herself that she had not previously known. There is more than lust in her longing looks. He does appear, of course, running through the crowds with a package for her, a parting gift; this love is complicated and so cannot drift to a happy ending we might expect or want. But in fact it is a happy ending. She is smiling and waving madly as the train leaves Venice, so much happiness, so much exultation, so much of feeling that all desires have been met.

⁕

A week later my train glided home along the coastline of the Irish Sea on the same route that I came in on. I was one of the few at the end of the train so I stood up to see the view, this pairing of railway and open water a daring engineering endeavour. I felt as though we could tumble into the sea, but it was excitement not fear I felt, my comfort zone long compromised. I would soon be back in Norwich, then move to the United States, and right then I was feeling as rootless as those seeds scattered up the country by the wake of the train.

The image of the seeds that spread across England, swirling and proliferating along train routes, have always seemed magical. My curiosity led me to speculate on where Druce's seed might have eventually taken root, what swish of a skirt or pant leg might have pushed it along and eventually brushed it away into the verge near the railway station. The next day's rain would then have forced it into the soil and a year later a sprout would emerge to produce more seeds that would be swept yet farther down the line. The seeds along railway tracks were not always welcome, especially those of trees, but they produced the most wonderful wild foliage.

Tycoons *and* Explorers

You cared neither for Gods nor grass, but for
cash (which you did not know the way to get);
you thought you could get it by what the Times
calls "Railroad Enterprise." You Enterprised
a Railroad through the valley—you blasted its
rocks away, heaped thousands of tons of shale
into its lovely stream. The valley is gone, and the
Gods with it; and now every fool in Buxton can
be in Bakewell in half an hour, and every fool in
Bakewell at Buxton; which you think a lucrative
process of exchange—you Fools Everywhere.

—John Ruskin, *Fors Clavigera: Letters to the*
Workmen and Labourers of Great Britain

It is the loss of the swimming girl that we talk about when my husband and I think back to the trip from Buffalo to New York on the Empire route. This four-inch figure in a two-piece striped red bathing suit with a happy smile was the portal to another world for my daughter. Hers was a rich imagination that would grow and blossom, creating a strong foundation for her adult inner life. It didn't start with swimming girl, but that's the point at which it registered with me. And now swimming girl was gone.

We'd boarded the train early at the suburban station of Depew on the overnight service from Chicago. Awakening bodies were sprawled over seats, blankets draped over armrests, backpacks gutted, chairs reclined, chip packets swirling around, so that we felt like intruders wandering into a camp already set up. But this was March, not peak time, and there was plenty of space so that our coach tickets felt like first class. Two double seats with leg rests across from one another, a sign that we would ride well.

We were already on the outskirts of Buffalo so we quickly entered the land of the farms and forests of upstate New York. We had driven this route and so recognized the names along the way, felt a certain ownership of places like Herkimer, where we had once lunched at a diner where they would spin a flashing carnival wheel to see who would get a free lunch, and the bread factory in Amsterdam near the bridge that spans only part of the river. We knew that Syracuse is halfway to Albany.

꘠

The Empire—the name itself evoking a distinct kind of attitude—had its origins when Cornelius Vanderbilt consolidated a number of lines in his rapidly growing business. Of course the story does not start with this acquisition. For that we have to go back to young Cornelius, who quit school when he was eleven to work with his father, then at sixteen borrowed money from his mother to start up his own ferry business between Staten Island and Manhattan, earning him the nickname "Commodore," which stuck to him for the rest of his life.

The ferrying business eventually led to the steamship business, which at that time in the United States, was the chief form of long-distance transportation. With every acquisition and transaction, Vanderbilt gained more security, and more property. When he owned the largest fleet of ships in the country, he recognized that trains would soon replace them and started investing in railroads. Expansion was in the cards in his domestic life as well. Having married his first cousin, Sophie, he would eventually father twelve children.

But this amassing of wealth is only one strand to Vanderbilt's life, and perhaps because it is a familiar story, it is the less interesting one. There were two open secrets that form different strands—the first that he had an insatiable sexual appetite, and the second that he was a strong believer in spiritualism and had his own advisor in a Mrs. Tufts. For years he regularly made the pilgrimage to Staten Island to visit Mrs. Tufts, who helped him commune with a variety of spirits including his mother and George Washington. For someone who might want to home in on a person's vulnerable spot, there was rich territory here, and when Mrs. Tufts had made enough money to retire to Vermont, Vanderbilt was left with no one to consult. The sisters Victoria Woodhull and Tennessee Claflin were only too willing to fill the void left.

Vanderbilt was the sort of man who insisted his barber collect and burn his hair to prevent someone from obtaining a lock and holding some power over him, and who put salt-cellars under the legs of his bed to ward off evil spirits, so it is easy to see how the sisters, each with their own sexual charm and a savviness in a range of spiritualist practices, would wield influence over him. Despite his wealth, when he met the sisters he was on the fringe of society, known for his excessive cursing and habit of spitting tobacco juice on the carpet of his host's home, and lonely, for his wife had just died.

I'm fascinated by how spiritualism and women's rights were intertwined in this period—both were responses to the control and subjugation of church and state—and it was clear that these two sisters held considerable power. Raised by a conman father, Buck Claflin, they were dabbling in mysticism as well as prostitution before they made their way to New York City, where they advertised as mediums who could speak to the dead. Tennessee, known as Tennie, soon became a fixture at Vanderbilt's home and saw to his corporeal needs by practising magnetic healing. There was talk of an affair. Her sister Victoria saw to his spiritual health by transmitting messages from the Commodore's dead mother. Having gained his trust, soon she was offering advice on business decisions. Though he didn't question whether her advice came from the spirit world or the real world, it is likely that she was tipped off by a friend who worked in the brothel frequented by men of business who liked to brag. In one move he declared an eighty percent stock dividend on the Central Pacific Railroad (issuing four extra shares for every five owned) and following advice he'd received from Victoria while in a trance, he told a young widow to place all her savings in Central. "It's bound to go up . . . Mrs. Woodhull said so in a trance." By the time the exchange closed, it had gone up to $165 from the opening of $134. Later, when she advised on gold trading that netted him a profit of $1.3 million just before Black Friday when the market collapsed, he was said to have given her half his profits.

Vanderbilt was planning to marry Tennie shortly after Sophie's death, when the Vanderbilt family brought up a distant cousin from Alabama, thirty-year-old Frank Armstrong Crawford. Vanderbilt eloped with her to Canada. As for Tennie and Victoria, he helped finance the sisters in setting up the first female stock brokerage. When that failed, they established themselves in the same office as publishers of the *Woodhull & Claflin's Weekly*, a political paper notorious for its coverage of sex education, women's suffrage, spiritualism, vegetarianism, and legalized sex work. The newspaper became the chief propaganda tool for Victoria Woodhull when she ran for president in 1872, the same year that the newspaper exposed an affair between the abolitionist Henry Ward Beecher and a friend's wife. The topic of adultery in print was deemed obscene by the New York commissioner, who had Woodhull imprisoned. She spent election day in jail.

When he died Cornelius left ninety-five percent of his wealth to his oldest son, William, but the will was contested by William's brothers and sisters on the grounds that their father had been ill-advised by a spiritualist. The allegation was that the spiritualist had been paid off by William to go into a trance during a session and tell Cornelius that his oldest son was the most trustworthy and that his other children hated him and were waiting for him to die to collect their share of the fortune. William didn't want to drag the family name through the courts so he eventually settled with his siblings.

In reading about this history, I could not help but notice the conjunction of this story of an empire-building, sex-greedy man who depended on advice from mediums to get through life, with the fact that the Empire travels through the heartland of the women's movement, Seneca Falls. Here there is a museum to mark the first convention of the women's rights movement, and in Rochester, also on this route, is where social reformer and women's rights activist Susan B. Anthony lived.

The muscle of a train pulling away from a station is like a nerve signal—*easy now, relax*—and the Empire seemed to live up to its name, the great hulking mass rumbling forward. The train with its empire-like seats—broad, deep, plush—had enough legroom that I could stretch my legs straight out, and in fact, there was even a leg rest so that we could nearly recline as we watched the New York countryside slide by. We kept an eye on our daughter, completely immersed in her swimming-girl world, her small voice drowned by the clatter of the train as she both narrated and managed the conversation between the two of them, pausing only to glance out the window at a cow, a deer, a bridge. At times she would pause for longer, staring out the window as if trying to figure out the next turn of plot.

We too were in our own world. Reclining in that capacious space, watching the intensity with which my daughter played was a study in creativity and focus. This was the concentration of a child who had not yet learned to be distracted, who later when she learned to read would scowl angrily, just as the girl in *The Little Princess* did when interrupted, having been torn so brutally from her book.

In our contemporary life, creativity, focus, and stillness are each in short supply. Yet I cling to the possibility of each, a little mind train I keep trying to jump on when I feel despair creeping in. This is the offering of travel, a chance to calm the mind. Something in us is reset, the stillness permission to let us go somewhere else, or to disappear into our imaginations, just like my daughter.

※

Once we got to Albany we had to change trains and when we'd boarded the second train, we realized we'd made a mistake in only having a light lunch on the earlier train, thinking we'd have dinner in the dining car on the last leg to New York. Instead we ate cardboard pizza in the snack car, the only option on offer.

This route follows the Hudson River all the way to New York City. The river is named after Henry Hudson, an Englishman who explored the area in 1609 when working for the Dutch East India Company and after whom Canada's Hudson Bay is named. It's ironic that they named this river after Hudson since he only "discovered" it when, in search of a channel through North America on his way to Asia, he made his way up as far as Albany, some 150 miles before realizing it was a mistake. To say nothing of the people who knew this river long before Hudson.

But I like to think that this must be the way of explorers, to take risks, to make mistakes. Like any traveller who has taken the wrong turn, it's easy to imagine the frustration, especially by the seamen, of yet another cul-de-sac.

I've been on the *Mary Rose*, a sixteenth-century ship, now a museum in Portsmouth Harbour in England, and so have a sense of the dark, cramped conditions in which these sailors lived. Above deck, they were required to climb shroud lines to the horizontal spars on which the sails were set to fix or adjust them, sometimes done in the midst of a howling storm. A fall from these spars was certain death. They slept wherever they could find a spot. After weeks at sea their meat would be

gone, their butter rancid, their beer sour, and the hard tack bis-
cuits—a staple on such voyages—reduced to dust because of
the weevils. As our train travelled along the picturesque river,
I imagined that this part of the journey must have been a lark
for Hudson's crew after the wild and unpredictable months
crossing the Atlantic. They would have been better fed by this
point, having topped up on meat and vegetables by trading
with the Mi'kmaq at a stopover in LaHave, Nova Scotia, where
they repaired a broken mast.

❧

The idea of exploration seems locked in some long-ago time,
with those early sailing ships at sea weeks, even months, in
search of what we now call continents. There was no room for
small ambition here, nor skittishness, or for that matter, seasickness. Because I am not brave, I often think of the torment of
these journeys: weevil-infested hard tack, rats sniffing around
at night, wild and unpredictable seas, but mostly it is the uncertainty that rattles me, sailing unknown seas to find unknown
lands. I am not adventurous despite my love of travelling, and
this lifestyle would require embracing the unpredictable. Not
for me to discover new lands, but rather to move at the pace of
an observer. That is why trains suit me, and long road trips.

If I were to romanticize those early sailing journeys, it
may be that I would have thrived after all. The pace and vistas
would allow me to watch the full spectrum of the sun by day,
the moon by night. I would have found a corner at the bow to
sit and watch for birds, signs of fish, while keeping one eye on
the activities of the crew. I might learn the workings of the sextant myself, dare to be hoisted in a bosun's chair to the crow's

nest to watch for the hazards of other ships or to sight land once we were close enough to catch a glimpse.

❧

I can picture this now because I am thinking of that journey to New York and how my daughter's imagination flourished, and how mine drifted, too, to think of things beyond the quotidian. It seems that if we remain still long enough, even when we are moving, we can return to a state of introspection where we can fantasize about voyages on seventeenth-century sailing ships.

Watching my daughter that day I could see how she was developing as an individual, providing clues of who she would be as an adult. When I was trapped at home, with just the memory of past trips to remind me of my pre-pandemic life, I could finally see the limits I had placed on my own imagination. It is no small thing, this mind wandering, for despite all the good it can do me, it can also lead me into all kinds of catastrophic thinking. When I am going through periods of stress I dream of being at sea— ocean liners riding wild waves, ferries that crash into a dock, sailing ships that lose their mast. Even asleep I am travelling.

❧

The train tracks that run along the Hudson River to New York are a microcosm of the history of travel in North America, where it was waterways more than the stagecoach that was the train's true antecedent.

In Europe the railway replaced an existing transportation system, mainly roads for stagecoach and horses, as well as waterways. This was the period of the Industrial Revolution, where in Europe it focussed on manufacturing textiles and other goods. The subsequent increased productivity had a huge impact on the less efficient artisanal culture as well as the highly developed travel culture. At the beginning of the nineteenth century in North America there was no developed culture of artisanship or travel. Here, where there was a surplus of resources and shortage of labour, the Industrial Revolution came later, with a focus on agriculture and transportation. The aim of developing transportation was on settlement, creating routes along the Atlantic coast and the waterways that led inward, along rivers and the Great Lakes. Rivers were the first connectors for those early boats, most prominently the canoe and the bateau, a shallow, flat-bottomed boat used in the fur trade. Sailboats and horse-powered ferry boats came along after, along with the canals. Travel writer G.T. Poussin noted of his travel journey in 1836: "One of the most curious circumstances is, no doubt, the abundance of its [America's] vast and navigable rivers, its great bays, straits and lakes, all of which contribute to a coherent interior navigation system incomparable to that of any other continent."

When Robert Fulton developed the sidewheel steamer in the early 1800s, unique in that it had two paddlewheels on either side amidships, as opposed to the rear-wheel version we associate with the Mississippi, he revolutionized travel in the United States. No longer reliant on wind or current, this boat, dubbed "Fulton's Folly," proved detractors wrong when it made a successful thirty-hour journey from New York to Albany. The 150-mile journey cost seven dollars, and while it only travelled at five miles an hour, it was much faster than its predecessor, a horse-powered ferry. By 1840, there were nearly one hundred steamboats on the Hudson River operated by various ferry lines, and competition was fierce, with Cornelius Vanderbilt in the midst of the scrum.

When the railroad came along offering speed and frequency, the steamboats changed course and the owners sought to appeal to those interested in leisure travel by transforming them into "floating palaces." They had dining rooms and saloons outfitted with hardwood furnishings, live music, a barbershop, electric lights, and one even had a darkroom where you could develop your photographs. The luxurious interior of the steamboat was seen by some to influence the later design of the railway car, and perhaps served as a prototype for the Pullman car in America, with its long and spacious saloon that offered the ability to walk around while underway.

The Hudson River, viewed by train, is vast and, in some places, still untamed. Houses cluster on the banks but there are stretches where there is nothing but wilderness, so you can see the river for the water highway it once was. And so it was that when we passed what we later learned was Bannerman Castle, a ruin on a small island in the river that we'd seen fleetingly, it was as if the past was a ghost waiting for us.

The remains of the castle dominate the small island of Pollepel, fifty miles north of New York City. It was built by Francis Bannerman, an immigrant from Scotland who started out collecting scrap metal in Brooklyn and built a munitions business that outgrew his base in Brooklyn. In the early 1900s, he designed the castle in the baronial style he'd seen on trips to Scotland; it would serve as a storehouse for his munitions business and a summer home for his family. Bannerman died in 1918, and in 1920 the powder house blew up, proving that the move from Brooklyn had been a good one. The explosion, fuelled by 200 tons of shells and powder, destroyed the edifice to the castle, though bizarrely, the family continued to live on the island until 1930, after which it began to fall into disrepair. A fire in 1969 reduced the castle to ruin.

~~&~~

There is no grand entry into New York City, rather a reel of graffiti-filled underpasses, side streets, and apartments that abut the track, until finally the train arrives in Penn Station, a labyrinthine crossroad that is all business, with travellers leaning into their march to the right exit, the next corridor. There is not the romance of the Grand Central Terminal that we would see a few days later, with its star-spangled cathedral vaulting and the bank of high windows through which shafts of sunlight would once pierce before the city was overtaken by the office towers that blocked the light.

Penn Station had its own days of glory. Built in 1910 on an eight-acre plot, 500 buildings were demolished to make way for the station, which would be considered a masterpiece in Beaux-Arts architecture when it was completed. By 1945, over a million passengers passed through it yearly, but the decline would come soon after with the surge in air travel and the building of inter-state highways. In 1954, the building's air rights were auctioned off, eventually making way for what would become Madison Square Gardens. The tracks, renovated concourse, and waiting room remained in place underground when demolition began in 1963 to international outrage, the catalyst for architectural preservation in the United States and the creation of the New York

City Landmarks Preservation Commission. In 1968, the owners of Grand Central Terminal began plans to demolish their station, but it was ultimately saved by the commission.

～✦～

In New York we went to the carousel in Central Park. Twice. Once to take our daughter, then the next day she took me because it was my birthday and she was four and so it made sense to her to take me to the carousel and then later to a café for cake—things that she adored. We walked the streets and looked at buildings and people, and visited bookstores and the Natural History Museum. We rode the subway at night and were only a little uneasy, and we visited parks when we came across them because slides and swings are the universal draw for a child. You see and travel through a city differently with children.

～✦～

At the hotel, I shot a video of our daughter as she entered her play world, singing "It Doesn't Matter," a song of her making that went on for a good five, maybe ten minutes. I watched it again recently as I was researching this book and I am convinced that there are lessons to be learned here: that we should shed all that is not important, the trivial, the ephemera of life, and that we should all metaphorically dance around on our beds singing made-up songs. I don't know what "didn't matter" to this four-year-old—was she being wise? Cheeky?

Covid lockdown was the time of no travel but it was also a time of endless calamity—political upheaval, racial tensions, economic collapse, with the climate crisis and the ever-changing pandemic a constant in our lives. We all had to learn what does or does not matter.

～🦎～

The night before we were to leave, we walked back to the hotel room to rest before dinner, and noticed a large tent attached to a building on the side street of our hotel. Curious, I walked over and asked a security guard what was going on. He told me that later they would premiere Martin Scorsese's Rolling Stones concert film, *Shine a Light* and the after-party was to be here.

Chuffed, we entered our hotel and walked towards the back of the lobby, to the bank of windows that faced the side street and the entrance to the night's party. We waited. We bought Pringles for our daughter because she was hungry and fidgety. We told her about movie directors and rock stars and soon she was in on the game. An hour passed. This was taking longer than we expected, but there was activity. People arriving, black cars pulling up and people getting out, but not famous people. More Pringles and a promise of spaghetti for dinner. Another black car pulled up and finally it was Martin Scorsese, not twenty feet away with nothing between us but the hotel glass. Then one by one, in their black cars, there was Mick Jagger, Keith Richards, Ron Wood, and Charlie Watts, and we were there with them.

～🦎～

Our adventure over, it was time to leave New York. When we boarded the train the next day we settled into our seats for the eight-hour return. We had lost swimming girl, but we'd acquired an Egyptian queen to replace her and our daughter would eventually build a world for her too.

The story of our trip to New York was one of world building—the wealth and might of entrepreneurs, the fantasy version of filmmakers and rock stars, the afterlife of spiritualists, the anticipated ones of explorers, and the wholly imagined ones of four-year-olds.

Pathologies:
Train Accidents
and Illnesses

It is really flying, and it is impossible to divest
yourself of the notion of instant death to all upon
the least accident happening.

—Thomas Creevey, English politician (1829)

I boarded the morning train to Montreal, bound for Moncton to visit family. I'd been away for some time, over a year in Poland, and I was going home for a month before starting a new job in Warsaw.

The train was full and the woman next to me was reading the newspaper, *The Sun*, and talking to me out of the side of her mouth about our loss of rights. Smoking being one of them. This was the early nineties, and it wasn't so long before that you could smoke on trains. That she didn't take into account the impact of secondhand smoke to non-smokers as the logic behind the new law was not something I thought necessary to raise. She saw this infringement as a signal of government overreach, perhaps even societal collapse.

I pulled my book out and buried myself deep into the pages.

Aside from her darting out to have a cigarette at designated stations, I paid little attention to her until, as we were approaching Montreal, the train came to a sudden stop. We were in a field of railway lines that ran parallel to us before converging at the upcoming station. We didn't move for some time, and we could tell from the frowns of the attendants that something had gone wrong.

The woman next to me began to get agitated. What's going on? she kept muttering. Why aren't we moving?

I could see that the issue of rights would soon come up. Now our right to arrive at a train station on time was being infringed. Her eyes darted outside, then up and down the aisle, and I soon realized that, like a true addict, she had timed her next cigarette and was holding on till she got to the final station. That plan had been scuppered.

The service attendants were evasive with information, but we soon learned that there had been a suicide on the tracks. Before long an ambulance arrived and we watched the paramedics carry the stretcher across the rows of tracks to our train. It felt like a long time between their disappearance from view and their reappearance, and in our suspended state of waiting, and grasping what had just happened, the car fell into a kind of reflective, respectful silence. Someone had died by the instrument on which we travelled. It was not our fault, to be sure, but that didn't change the fact that it had happened and I imagined that the others, like me, were trying hard to push the image of what the ambulance attendants were dealing with out of their minds.

Still, the woman beside me remained feral. She roamed the aisle, badgered the service manager, muttered to me, until finally we saw the rescue team stepping carefully across rails.

That stopped her for the moment. I watched as they carried the stretcher to the waiting ambulance, an exposed boot dangling from beneath the sheet.

If asked, I would say that my state of mind on train journeys is one of the relaxed daydreamer. I am a worrier and have a gift for anxiety, so when I board a train, I notice immediately the release of all that I normally hold on to. My shoulders drop, my body slumps into the seat, I can write, read, think, often with more intensity than I can at home. I'm often surprised that others don't think this way. Doesn't everyone find the train to be a form of retreat?

Because I've made the assumption that the train is a place of quietude for others too, and also that this has always been the case, I was surprised to learn that many passengers were in a constant state of fear in the early days of train travel. Speed put many travellers on edge, and adding the constant jolting of steel wheels on steel rails it became, as it is for some air travellers today, a white-knuckle experience.

For the unlucky, a constant state of nervous fear was justified. At 3:13 p.m. on June 9, 1865, a train travelling from Folkestone to London, England, crashed, killing ten people and injuring forty others. Known as the Staplehurst rail accident, the train derailed while crossing a viaduct where track had been removed for repair, and insufficient notice had been given to stop the train. The foreman had misread the schedule, which changed with the tides of the English Channel. The Tidal Express Service originated in Boulogne, France, with a boat train picking up ferry passengers at Folkestone in England. The train was unable to stop in time because the flagman was only 554 yards away, rather than the regulation 1,000 yards. This accident was notable, not just for the deaths and injuries that resulted, but also because Charles Dickens had been on board with his mistress, Ellen Ternan, and her mother.

In a letter to his friend, the solicitor Thomas Mitton, Dickens described the impact. "Suddenly we were off the rail, and beating the ground as the car of a half-emptied balloon might do."

His travelling companions screamed, to which he urged, "We can't help ourselves, but we can be quiet and composed. Pray don't call out." The carriage came to a halt, tilting down in one corner, and Dickens assured them that the worst was over. But when he crawled out of the carriage and onto the step, he could see the bridge was gone, leaving nothing below him but the tracks. He called to one of the guards, got the keys to his carriage, and freed his mistress and her mother. Once on land, he used his brandy flask to help comfort the wounded and his travelling hat as a basin that he filled with water from the river below to help wash the blood from other travellers. He gave one woman lying against a tree a drink of brandy before moving on to another passenger. When he passed by her again, she was dead.

Later he remembered that the manuscript of *Our Mutual Friend* was in the compartment and clambered back in to retrieve it.

A few days later in his letter to Mitton, Dickens wrote that he did not want to be part of the inquest, and he did not want to write about it. Despite the newsworthy potential of his presence on board, a lengthy report in *The Observer* makes minimal reference to him. "Mr. Charles Dickens had a narrow escape. He was in the train, but, fortunately for himself and for the interests of literature, received no injuries whatever." Given his fame and the fact that he tended to the injured, one could expect that more attention would have been paid. But Dickens was travelling with his mistress, and it's believed he wanted to protect his reputation, so he did not want to make much of his presence. This also could explain why he would not want to be part of the inquest. At the end of the letter, he tells Mitton that he was not in the least bit affected at the time, though his tone suddenly shifts. "But in writing these scanty words of recollection I feel the shake and am obliged to stop."

Dickens believed he was not affected at the time of the accident, but it is apparent that he suffered "railway shock," as it was then known—a precursor to shell shock and post-traumatic stress disorder—and it would continue to plague him in the years that followed. Dickens would thereafter be uneasy travelling by train, and avoided it where possible. He died five years later on the anniversary of the crash.

※

In 1862, *The Lancet*, the leading English medical journal, published a pamphlet called *The Influence of Railway Travelling on Public Health*, such were the concerns around this new mode of travel. It stated that there is a "condition of uneasiness, scarcely amounting to actual fear, which pervades the generality of travellers by rail. The possibility of collision is constantly present to such persons, and everyone knows how, if by chance a train stops at some unusual place, or if the pace be slackened, or the whistle sounds its shrill alarm, a head is projected from nearly every window, and anxious eyes are on the look-out for signs of danger."

The pamphlet also acknowledged that the swift pace of the train didn't allow for the restful observation of the scenery. The overtaxed eyes from rapid flickering images, the constant noise, the swaying and jolting, were all considered contributors to the psychic strain of travellers that was being studied by the best minds of the medical profession.

Speed was a primary concern; it was felt that women's bodies in particular were not built to travel fifty miles an hour and there was fear that their uteruses would fly out of their bodies as it reached that pace. Others felt that the human body would melt at such speed.

This was in the early days, of course, and can be seen as part of the normal concern about innovation. It's understandable that the speed was frightening (it was a new experience, after all), but also I imagine it was extremely exhilarating to others.

✦

In 1895, pioneering filmmakers Auguste and Louis Lumière made the short film *L'arrivée d'un train en gare de La Ciotat* (*The Arrival of a Train at La Ciotat Station*), a fifty-second silent film of a train entering a station while passengers waited on the platform. Legend has it that the impression of the train coming towards the audience was so powerful that audience members jumped up and ran to the back of the theatre, afraid that the train was actually coming through the screen. As this was one of the first moving pictures, it's seen as a significant part of film history. The hearsay around audience reaction to the film also speaks to the ever-present fear of trains, their might and power made forcefully evident by this locomotive bursting across the screen. The filmmakers were guaranteed a hit given how skittish people were about the new technology of both film and trains. It was indeed a success with journalists, amazed at the seemingly three-dimensional movement onscreen.

This famous story of the panicked reaction to the film has been repeated by film historians and writers over the years but has been rejected by Martin Loiperdinger, a film scholar at the University of Trier, Germany. "The moving images projected onto the screen with the Cinematographe Lumière could hardly be mistaken for reality," writes Loiperdinger. "Contemporary reports of panic reactions among the audience cannot be found." This film, now regarded as foundational to the medium's history, tapped into a vulnerability the public felt about the burgeoning technology of this new "iron horse" and awe at the sensory experience of moving pictures.

There is no definitive way of knowing the audience reaction, but what was true was an incident that took place two months before the screening, a runaway locomotive at the Montmartre Station in Paris broke through a second-storey wall and plummeted down into the street. Would this have been on the mind of those patrons attending the screening?

⚓

There was reason to be fearful in those early days. There were numerous accidents due to faulty equipment—railroads in the United States had limited regulations and early investors were driven by profits and not safety imperatives. This was a developing technology and, as such, changes only came through gradual engineering improvements or through regulation following catastrophic events.

Before effective signalling was in place, trains ran into each other, they flew off the rails because they were going too fast or there were objects on the lines or shoddily built railbeds had sunk into the soil. Survivors of these accidents often reported psychological distress, what we would now call PTSD. But there was also an aspect of survivors' anxiety and sleeplessness that was called "railway spine" or "railway brain" because autopsies indicated that railway accidents could cause microscopic lesions on the central nervous system, similar to damage done by whiplash.

Passengers, too, could be at fault. Some slipped off the platform, others were hit when leaning too far out the window, and a few even jumped to reclaim dropped parcels or hats. And there were those who were struck down in accidents at level crossings.

These accidents were regularly written about in the press, with *The Times* in London reporting a roundup under the heading "Friday's railway accidents" in September 1873, for example. The fact that all of these incidents were given generous coverage by the press could explain why there was widespread unease with train travel.

Queen Victoria was included among those apprehensive of train travel, though after taking a trip with her husband, Albert, the train became part of her life, allowing her to work while travelling. But she remained anxious about speed and set a limit of forty miles per hour. This was her way of coping, by maintaining control of the situation. It was similar to her pathological aversion to overheated rooms in her home, where she insisted that the temperature never exceeded fifteen degrees Celsius.

There was a period in Victorian England when the neurosis and nervous shock that travellers experienced went even further, during the phenomenon known as the "madmen on the train."

There were reported cases of men with no previous history of mental illness who would board the train and, once subjected to the rolling experience of movement and noise, fall into a form of mania. Professor Amy Milne-Smith, a cultural historian at Wilfrid Laurier University notes in her book *Out of His Mind: Masculinity and Mental Illness in Victorian England* "Stories of madmen on the railways were so frequent in the mid-1860s that one can identify a media panic." Trains were thought to injure the brain, with the jarring of the carriage likely to unhinge the mind and trigger some sort of outburst. As Milne-Smith writes, "In some cases, it seemed the train itself could cause the madness." Dickens calculated that the London to Edinburgh train would subject a passenger to 30,000 individual shocks to the nerves. One Scottish aristocrat travelling by train removed his clothes and began ranting out his window. When the train stopped he became completely composed again and disembarked. The "railway madmen" were such a concern during the 1860s and 1870s that some especially nervous American travellers took to carrying a gun when boarding British trains.

Another, perhaps even greater strain reported in *The Lancet* pamphlet was the "excitement, anxiety, and nervous shock consequent on the frequent efforts to catch the last express; to be in time for the fearfully punctual train." The introduction of train time, where schedules had to be learned and adhered to, added a new dimension of stress for travellers. Sigmund Freud would arrive at a station at least an hour before it was due to depart for fear of missing the train, and he was not alone in this particular neurosis. Anyone wishing to travel by train was forced to get used to the rigid structure of the newly imposed "railway time" that moved people away from various local times to a standard time in order to have a coordinated national schedule.

The idea of being hurried to death seems peculiar to us now in what we consider a fast-paced world, but the impact was much discussed through both anecdotal evidence and learned medical observation. The speed of train travel was blamed for unexpected births or miscarriages—Dickens's wife among those who suffered a miscarriage on a train.

It also was held responsible for deteriorating health and in some unfortunate cases, death. In 1868, Dr. Alfred Haviland wrote the publication *"Hurried to Death": or, a few words of advice on the Danger of Hurry and Excitement, especially addressed to Railway Travellers*, in which he observed that season-ticket-holders on the Brighton line aged more quickly than non-travellers, and also noted the danger to those rushing to catch their train who might have an undetected illness exacerbated by this frenzied dash. The case of a thirty-five-year-old fishmonger who ran to catch his train and immediately died upon sitting into his seat was given as one example of evidence of this phenomenon.

In the period of the great pause, when the pace of many of our lives slackened, there was talk that this is the way it would be from now on, a gearing down, a new appreciation for slow travel. For those of us who felt adrift in our homes, no plans to make, there was an untethered existence we thought we'd learn from. No more racing here and there for us, we thought.

Time will offer perspective, but the signs were telling as we re-entered our lives, not with some timidity, as expected, but with great speed. So eager was our return that we forgot what those days of reflection had revealed. That we were adaptable. That our way of living, our way of thinking was not as static as we might have believed. And we would soon learn that this temporary conditioning for slow that we had undergone could easily fall away. How easy it was, both in our bodies and in our minds, to return to a quickened pace. We could not adopt a nineteenth-century bucolic lifestyle as we had become too accustomed to the modern day version of "fast travel" that technology had normalized. We travelled back in time for those years and now are speeding towards the future. We won't know whether this will change us and if so, how, for some time, I expect.

In the generations since the early days of train travel, we have grown accustomed, both physically and mentally, to the technology of travel. We now take trains as a matter of course, bracing ourselves against their jostling, thinking it part of the charm as we scan the passing scenery. Indeed, we now think that we are undertaking "slow travel," and the environmentally friendly option at that, whereas in the early days, in England in particular, trains were seen as tearing up the landscape, the tracks destroyers of rural beauty.

So how is it that we have shifted the manner in which we experience train travel from that of our forebears? How has their fast become our slow?

⤛⁂⤜

We'll soon be there, I told the woman, who had finally settled back in her seat beside me. We had started to move again, and everyone was fidgeting as they packed up whatever they'd brought to see them through the trip.

I've missed my connection, she scowled at me, seemingly unaware that many were in the same position.

I can still hear that woman's voice, her discontent like a badge of honour. Had the government taken away her right to be happy too? First the smoking, and then the inconvenience of someone's death. It seemed not to matter to her that sometimes we need to think beyond ourselves, beyond our own needs. This woman's resentment resonated anew as our pandemic world closed in further, and further still. The second wave, the third, the fourth, the now unnumbered, where the wearing of masks and the requirement to vaccinate in the name of public health and the common good have become a question for some, of rights. The defiant minority, not so silent.

Everything seemed a danger in the days of lockdown, travel included, but not in the way our ancestors considered it. The danger our forebears felt was in some ways real given that the technology was still new, and indeed, still developing, but it was also somewhat fabricated fear because they were still getting accustomed to this ferocious speed and the implied hazard.

In our pandemic time there were those who ignored the warnings and continued to board trains, and planes for that matter, to holiday destinations, unconcerned about the potential danger the virus might inflict, as though this was a right, no matter the risk to others. At the same time, there were those who had no choice in facing this imperilment, either for work, or to see family members. This, to my mind, raises the question of whether travel is a right or a privilege. The answer may be complicated but it's one I reflected on a lot during lockdown, when the trips I'd planned had to be cancelled. I hadn't thought much about it in the past, taking for granted my ability to go when and where my means allowed, whether a spontaneous hitchhiking trip to Halifax in my university days, or the annual trip to England to see my in-laws. Will I think of travel as a right after all this, or a privilege? I think I've figured it out.

The Train
Station

The railway stations are the places where
England is most openly gloomy. Scrap iron
piles up there and coal dust and heaps of
rusting, tangled and disused rails. They are
surrounded by desolate little allotments full
of cabbages where bits of underwear are hung
out to dry and where there are sheds patched
together like old sheets.

—Natalia Ginzburg, *The Little Virtues*

If you walk into the main entrance to Valencia's North Train Station in Spain and look up, you will see panels of inlaid mosaic work in the trencadís technique. Trencadís, a Catalan term that means chopped, was an artform popularized by Antoni Gaudí, the eccentric genius behind the famed Sagrada Família in Barcelona. It is achieved by cementing together irregular pieces of marble, glass, or ceramic tiles. Here in this station, the ceiling is a sea of creamy mosaic pieces with flourishes at each end of the individual panels.

As your eyes drift down to the walls of the concourse, you'll see that they are clad in mosaic as well, though of a different colour, a pale mauve. This contrasts beautifully with the dark wood that surrounds the ticket wickets along one wall. In the middle of the room there are two circular wooden benches with a column in the centre of each against which you can rest your back. Directly above are five light globes hanging from rods, perhaps to provide enough illumination to check the time of your train if you found yourself there at night.

Of course, if you have purchased your ticket online you might walk through this hall with just a fleeting admiring glance, as I have done when running late. But if you pause and look around, you will see that it is as timeless as a museum, so much so that you can imagine the people who have travelled through here, people like Ernest Hemingway, who entered the station in 1925, drawn to Valencia to see the bullfights. On that day he was heading next door to the Plaza de Toros to watch one. Hemingway settled in Valencia for a year while he wrote *The Sun Also Rises* and over his lifetime would frequent the station often, returning in 1936 to the city while covering the Spanish Civil War, and again in 1959 on assignment for *Life* magazine. The city is referred to in seven of his novels, and it's been estimated that he visited the bullfights at the Feria de San Jaime fifteen times. It was a city that never lost its appeal for him.

This is not the first North Station built in Valencia; the initial one was a ten-minute walk away, in what now is a square in front of the town hall. Valencia had fortified walls dating from the eleventh century, so when a railway was contemplated in 1847, the first obstacle was the wall itself. A gap was cut in the curtain wall so that trains could enter the city, but was torn down completely in 1865 and replaced with the boulevard now known as Calle Jativa. The original station was soon deemed too small so planning began for a larger one. The location of the station we use today is on the other side of Calle Jativa. However, the problem when building it was that it would be in the path of the old one. The solution was to make an opening in the new station while under construction to allow the trains to continue through. Finding gaps for trains seems to have been an ongoing problem in Valencia.

Historic pictures of the station show that the opening for the trains is where today we enter and leave the building, slightly to the left of what would appear to be the main doors. While this station was being built, a train would have to come through there and then cross the busy Calle Jativa into the square now filled with people. It requires a leap in imagination, and offers insight into the problem-solving minds of engineers. I'm sure they wished for a simpler solution.

❦

We arrive in Valencia from the south, having taken the train from the small station in Xeraco, an hour away. We approach the city after travelling through orange groves and suburbs of apartment complexes. We are a group of eight, two families who have done this trip many times. Our rhythms are in sync, thanks to a friendship that has flourished and deepened, one that has become essential over the years. We travel as a unit and are practiced at packing sandwiches, snacks, books, water. We read or look out the window on this brief trip that takes us from the region of La Safor mountain range, where we are based, to the city. Because we often plan this day out when rain is forecast, thinking it will be a relief from the hot sun, we have seen some spectacular stormy skies from the train window.

The train shuttles in on one of the six tracks under the large cantilevered dome that extends from the main station building and covers the platforms and the large concourse area, where we will return to stand and wait for our train at the end of the day. Conceived in 1907, the cantilevered dome, with a height of eighty-two feet and a span of a hundred forty-eight feet, was another engineering achievement. It was constructed in Madrid and transported and erected in parts. When completed, it had electrically controlled windows that ensured good ventilation against the steam from the trains below. The dimensions of this station were a source of great pride at the time since it was larger than that of other European cities such as Paris, Berlin, and Vienna.

We walk out of the station to the ceramic-tiled plaza and see the city of Valencia, a mix of old, such as the brick bullfighting ring to our right, and new, with the row of clothing shops across the street—the pairing seamless in a city that seems eager to make an impression. This is the way you should enter or exit the portal of travel, through a corridor of beauty, with a lingering story of its past, and a sense of slow and melancholic ease.

~❦~

Once when I was young, I was told that I had an old soul. Because I was not very old at the time, perhaps in my twenties, I thought it somehow was connected to being old and found it an odd statement. Consequently I ignored it. It wasn't until some years ago when someone called my daughter, then barely ten, an old soul that I remembered.

I don't know if I'm really an old soul but I do know that I have a deep connection to place, and an abiding interest in history that helps explain how I—and we—exist in the world. I have a tendency to look backwards for wisdom. No one would accuse me of being a visionary. So I appreciate those who, when designing places such as this station, take into account a traveller's wellbeing, their wish to be enchanted. It is just a place to pass through, I know, but its significance seems to pull at something in me, a merging of place and history. And I often find myself observing the others who travel through this crossroad with me, and I imagine their reunions, fresh starts, homecomings. The curiosity in me wants to know their backstories.

Although there are some stations that do not spur my imagination in the way that Valencia does.

I've been mulling over the train stations I've passed through, and it is the Montreal Central station that most comes to mind. I am weighed down when I think of the many arrivals I've made there.

Coming from the west, the train curves in towards Montreal's downtown skyline, and there, high above on one of the buildings, we can see the large CN logo that marks our destination. There is a sense of a bunched-together skyline, and the slow ambling pace of the train makes it feel as though we are sauntering in, that we have a right to be there. That is, until we get to the station, where we are taken into our subterranean platform as if shuttled in undercover.

Here, at the arrival point, the lights are low, and so too it seems, is the ceiling. Rather than feeling elevated at this arrival, there is a sense of gloom. The train comes to a stop and we step onto the platform to be met with the smell of cement dust and diesel, and I have to resist the urge to cover my nose and mouth as we pause in the queue of people waiting to go up the escalator or stairs.

We are anxious to get to the upper level, for some fresh air, to a lofty ceiling that does not trick us into stooping as we walk. This upper level is spacious, the ceiling expansive, and a bank of windows at the end offers some natural light, but still there is an air of functionality about the architecture, the style of which was hailed as "modern" and "international" when it opened in 1946. Construction began in 1929 but was halted in 1930 for nine years during the Depression. The station was always intended to take into consideration the "air rights" as a potential for development, much the same way as Penn Station and Grand Central Station in New York. Air rights had been long under pressure at urban train stations. At one time it had been necessary to keep the area above the tracks open to allow sufficient ventilation for the steam trains below. With electric and diesel taking over this was no longer needed, and air rights became valuable real estate released for development, especially in the United States. This explains why in Grand Central Station the grandeur can only be seen in the upper levels, while the trains themselves remain in the dull basement beneath their midtown high-rises, much like Montreal.

In the early days, urban stations were seen as city gateways because this was the main route in or out for most travellers. They were also a gateway in the sense of easing the traveller into this "industrialized space," as train stations were considered then, a necessary transition from the slow pace of the city to the speed of the trains. The entry point for pedestrians was the reception building that faced the city, usually the grandest part of the station, where people would purchase tickets and wait for their train. There was no direct access to the platforms and travellers were kept in a holding area, much as we wait at a gate for an airplane today.

For the trains, entry was through the train shed, a building adjacent to a train station that faced the countryside and covered the tracks and platforms with an overarching roof, often steel and glass, to house the trains. The term "shed" is an understatement carried over from the original makeshift canopy on two iron columns built at the Liverpool Station in England, and the name has stuck, now representing many feats of architectural and engineering marvel, such as that cantilevered roof structure at the Valencia station.

In Europe the stations were often built outside city limits, and were viewed for a long time as industrial and proletarian, a stigma that caused their surrounding areas to be known as the disreputable "railway district." In the United States, where the stations were in the city centre much like the stagecoach depots had been, the tracks divided the city so that one side held the wealthier citizens, while the other featured factories and worker tenements, becoming known as "the wrong side of the tracks."

⚜

When travelling on the Ocean from Montreal to Moncton, we make twenty-two stops along the route and most are small rural stations, utilitarian in design—one large room with a ticket office, waiting room, and perhaps a refreshment stand.

The station at Jacquet River in New Brunswick, as I mentioned earlier, appears in an opening in the trees with little sign of a settlement. Its plain wooden structure and its location makes it feel abandoned, and indeed whenever we've stopped, there is rarely more than one or two cars in the parking lot, the waiting passengers standing on the platform or sitting in their cars. Because this is the hamlet where my mother grew up, I always pause to look out, and sometimes I've been in the observation car, where I can look down the track and see the isolation of this location. Indeed, it seems to come into existence only by the fact of our being there, a kind of Brigadoon.

The poet Edward Thomas was inspired by the simple structure and the isolation of such stations, though his were in England. He wrote about such stations in the poem "Adlestrop," which was a weatherboard building with a booking hall and office on one side, a waiting room on the other, fitting into an area barely thirty feet long, with no pretensions of architectural style.

The steam hissed. Someone cleared his throat.
No one left and no one came
On the bare platform. What I saw
Was Adlestrop—only the name . . .

Philip Larkin wrote of a livelier spectacle in "The Whitsun Weddings." The narrator is a traveller who observes families gathering at the platforms along the line from the east of England to London, seeing off brides and grooms who have chosen this popular day to get married. Each station becomes the send-off point to the rest of their lives, the platform almost an extension of the reception and the wedding itself.

> And banquet-halls up yards, and bunting-dressed
> Coach-party annexes, the wedding-days
> Were coming to an end. All down the line
> Fresh couples climbed aboard: the rest stood round;
> The last confetti and advice were thrown . . .

Perhaps the origins of trains' allure for me come from my great-grandfather, a station master who lived with his wife above a station in northern New Brunswick. She was by all accounts a difficult woman who rode the train to sell Avon products to neighbouring communities. I'm told he was a quiet man, and a reader. My aunt tells me you could ask him the meaning of any word and he would know it, despite his limited education. He was always reading, she said. That's what they said about me as a child.

I like to think he had a peaceful time of it, working at that station, his wife away selling makeup and perfumes, and at the end of the day, his duties done, he could sit and read a book. I'm idealizing this of course, as monotony must have been part of it, and perhaps loneliness. The accommodations, I imagine, were basic, probably just a few rooms above the station.

Such living arrangements were not unusual for station masters in rural outposts on both sides of the Atlantic, and sometimes in larger stations there were accommodations for the head porter as well. Like the pastor who lived in the rectory, it meant stability, respectability, a solid standing in the community. The station master had to oversee the running of the trains, check the facilities on a daily basis, supervise staff, deal with complaints, and then there was the paperwork. One station master in Templecombe, England, wrote in 1912 that his day began at 7:45 a.m. when he would have between fifty to a hundred letters waiting for his response. The letters came from head office, or staff, or other station masters and might range from specific instructions for the day, to complaints, to arrangements for a child travelling alone.

Not everyone was suited to this life, of course, and included in those whose calling was elsewhere was Branwell Brontë, brother of the famous Brontë sisters. He was hired as station master at Luddendenfoot in 1840 at an annual salary of £130. He spent the lonely hours at work between trains sketching his colleagues and writing verses. As soon as the last train had gone, he would head to the nearby inn to read and, perhaps, find conversation. Then he began taking off before the last train, leaving his porter to issue tickets and keep the books. When the annual audit was conducted, they were short over eleven pounds and the ledger had scribbles and sketches all over it. Both Branwell and the porter were fired and the amount missing deducted from Branwell's outstanding salary.

The uniform, too, was often a measure of community standing. In the Czech film *Ostře sledované vlaky* (*Closely Watched Trains*), the first several minutes are of a young man being assisted by his mother as he dresses in his uniform for his first day of work at the train station. It's as if he's just joined the military. Wool trousers, white shirt, a jacket that featured a stand-up collar with decorative motifs, and a long woollen coat. As an apprentice, he gained status with this uniform, just as his station master, who lived above the station with his wife, lost some when his uniform became sullied by the pigeons he kept, speaking to them as pets while brushing droppings and feathers from his jacket. Later, he is shown being measured by a tailor for a new bespoke uniform.

Some station masters planted gardens, the more ambitious arranging the station's name in flowers. Although station gardens started in England, they became popular in Canada as a way of beautifying the somewhat drab environment in what was becoming a community hub. It also encouraged agricultural settlement and tourism, the lush gardens indicating a rich and fertile soil beyond the station. The gardens, tended by staff, were also used to encourage morality, as drunkenness among railway employees was an increasing problem. As one Canadian newspaper noted, "a man with a beautiful garden is a man who does not waste time in taverns or with a pipe in his mouth nor is he a man who beats his wife or neglects his children."

As gardens caught on it became a custom to exchange seeds up and down the line. The Canadian Pacific Railway (CPR) encouraged station gardens and in some cases there were garden competitions. In 1896, Station Constable Robillard, who was in charge of the gardens in Ottawa, considered acquiring a gun to take care of the hens who were picking at his prized flowers.

In 1907, a forestry department was established within CPR to take care of the gardens, and greenhouses were set up in several centres. A floral department was also established, and by 1910 they were tending to 1,500 gardens. In 1911 alone, 100,000 packets of flower seeds were delivered to the stations. As they expanded west the gardens became a gateway and an advertisement directed at new immigrants for the flourishing life they could expect on the Prairies. During World War I, many added vegetable gardens to their plots to help with the war effort, and it was estimated that eventually one-third of railway gardens in Canada were devoted to potatoes.

W.M. Winegar, CPR representative at the time, understood the impression an entry point can make on a traveller. He said that a traveller having been positively influenced will later say, "I remember that town, there must be a fine spirit there, the station was neat and the garden well kept, and the surroundings attractive."

❧

To me train stations encapsulate anticipation, travellers standing on the platform looking down the line, searching for the headlights that means the train will soon be there. It could be the start of a journey or the expectation of being reunited with a friend or loved one. In the David Lean film *Brief Encounter*, the anticipation is of romance: two lovers meet weekly at the station before leaving on separate trains. It was filmed in 1945 at Carnforth Station because it was far enough from German airfields that blackout rules could be relaxed. The nighttime shots are atmospheric, with great plumes of steam, an odd lightbulb here and there that throws light and shadow on the platform as travellers rush to catch their trains. Inside the tea shop are those still waiting to depart. The lovers meet there and sit at a table picking at a bun, a cup of tea, or a brandy if it is after six.

❧

At the end of the day in Valencia we are back at North Station, perhaps stopping at the café for a drink while we wait. Some in our group will dash off to the sweet shop on one side, others to the Ale-Hop store, a favourite in which to browse for fun trinkets. We are tired from walking, some of us are carrying bags with new purchases, and we linger in the middle of the concourse, waiting to go through to our train, this beautiful hall a welcome space that allows us to separate from the day in the city and prepare for our journey back.

In that time of lockdown when this trip was cancelled two years running I adopted some magical thinking, transporting myself at will to that station, to the start of that day, our train pulling in under the grand cantilevered roof. In my mind I walk with our group past the turnstiles, and out into the open concourse that is never terribly crowded even in the summer. The sounds of sandals slapping against the ceramic floor, or the hard tap of a shoe, the smell of machinery grease, the natural lighting, the light breeze that drifts through, the discreet signs of commercialism are comforting to me as we are about to embark on our day in the city.

When I am standing in that concourse in the roof's shade, readying myself to enter the city, it is as though the building's elegance enhances an inner style I didn't know I had. I somehow feel elevated by being there. It is just a passage point, but it has such grace and artfulness that it allows me to go through some form of transformation myself.

We drift through stations all the time, but the manner in which we do so matters—it allows us to enter the rest of our journey on the right footing, in a settled peace of mind. We can think to ourselves: I have arrived.

The Extraordinary Ordinary:
Ways *to* Travel

*I feel a thrill that is very like fear; but it is
gone at once, and I can think of nothing but the
novelty, the excitement, and the fun of this mad
ride in glorious sunshine and intoxicating air,
with magnificent mountains before and around
me, their lofty peaks smiling down on us, and
never a frown on their grand faces!*

—Lady Agnes Macdonald as she rode the
cowcatcher through the Rocky Mountains for
six hundred miles while her husband, John A.
Macdonald, remained in their private train car

I magine, as I have, waking up in a train buried in snow. The banked coal fire keeping you warm, a stillness that only a world buffered by snow can create. Now imagine that this is no ordinary train, but one with the kind of luxury usually reserved for royalty. A lounge with sofas and club chairs, an upright piano, potted palms, and bouquets of flowers. The car itself inlaid with wood panelling, brass lamps, velour draperies, stained glass windowpanes, carpets, and zebra rugs. An adjoining dining room holds a table for ten and is served by two cooks. It is a train with two sleeping rooms, and your own has a large brass bed and a carved mahogany vanity.

Now imagine you are Sarah Bernhardt, the French actress, and it is Christmas Day in 1880 and you are marooned on this train just outside of Urania, Michigan. It is the middle of a six-month tour, and your decision to make a detour to do a private performance in Ann Arbor on Christmas Eve now seems a grave error in judgment.

Snow was already falling when Bernhardt gave her performance, and the railroad superintendent, concerned that the recently completed rail line from Ann Arbor to Toledo would be covered in snow for her return journey the next morning, ordered another train—a locomotive, three empty boxcars, and a caboose—to clear the track. Train travel during the nineteenth century in the loosely regulated United States was often a rugged affair with the threat of gangs plundering cars, bridges unable to hold the weight of the train, and tracks that had been hastily put down in the westward expansion. Bernhardt, aware of these dangers, would speak to the local engineer before any trip to make sure he was reliable and was known to send a tip up to him at the end of the journey.

For this American tour, Bernhardt had prepared a repertoire of eight plays, the most popular being *The Lady of the Camellias*. Although most Americans were unable to understand the plays that were performed entirely in French, they were drawn to the visual spectacle of it, and of course to her reputation. Known as "The Bernhardt," people flocked to see her, this woman reputed to have many paramours and oozing an exoticism that was both naughty and alluring.

Two trains were required for the six-month tour. One, a freight train, hauled the significant baggage and equipment needed for the shows. The other was dubbed the "Sarah Bernhardt Special" and comprised three Pullman cars with sleeping accommodations for the troupe and a fourth that was the luxurious "palace car" reserved for Bernhardt.

It's not known who the private performance in Ann Arbor was for, but she left many of her actors behind for the Christmas Eve event, selecting just a few to join her, along with the required props and costumes. There was a plan to return to Toledo to rejoin the rest of the troupe on Christmas Day.

When Bernhardt's train set off there seemed little to worry about, but Urania Hill, just ten miles outside of Ann Arbor, would most certainly have been on the engineer's mind. There was a railcut that sliced through the hill and created a narrow valley susceptible to drifting snow. On this day, although the track had been cleared, snow was quickly filling in again. As the train approached Urania Hill, the fireman built up steam to take on the incline that the cut had not completely eradicated. It made it halfway before coming to an abrupt stop.

It's hard to imagine what that moment of impact would have been like for Bernhardt, whom I've pictured resting in one of the club chairs, or on a sofa, perhaps having a cup of tea. The cooks might have been preparing lunch, the others in the troupe playing a game of cards, while outside snow swirled and swooped down on them.

Then, bang! A snow wall. Glasses knocked over, brass lamp swaying, a book dropped on the floor. Silence.

What they wouldn't immediately know is that the Bernhardt Special train was eighteen inches wider than standard cars, and although the way had been cleared as instructed, it had not been wide enough for her train. And so it became wedged, as the conductor, Donovan, put it, "like a cork in a bottle."

❧

Despite the glamour cast by Bernhardt, this story is actually rooted in the very practical need to get around America for work. Steamship and stagecoach would have been the only other options, so trains such as hers served as a private jet does now. Or for the less moneyed, the tour bus.

The need to be somewhere, to get somewhere, has made the train relevant from the beginning, but the question of how to get where we're going has changed considerably.

When trains first became popular, there was much comparison to the steamboat it was quickly replacing. However, while the steamboat described in the 1840 *Merchants' Magazine and Commercial Review* as "saloons with gilded columns, carpeted with the costly fabrics of foreign looms, adorned with mirrors and paintings and rich tapestry," thus inspiring the term "steamboat gothic," the train of that era had no reasonable luxurious counterpart. That is until George Pullman came along, and the previously classless American rail system introduced "first class," reflecting the nation's growing wealth. The United States was expanding west and the desire for comforts on these long journeys became apparent. George Pullman, an engineer and industrialist who took over his father's business (a firm that, through the senior Pullman's invention, could jack up buildings along the Erie Canal and move them back so it could be widened), was a frequent train traveller. He rued the hard seats and limited amenities of train cars and decided to do something about it. The result was a more developed sleeping car consisting of an upper sleeping berth that could be pushed up into the ceiling compartment and seats that could convert into a lower berth. Draperies and washrooms on the car were another welcome addition to what became known as the Pullman car.

Comfort and design marked the Pullman trains, but they were equally noted for their Black porters. George Pullman himself travelled to the south to recruit formerly enslaved men to work on the railroad. His vision for the Pullman experience included providing first-class service for middle-class travellers, something they were unaccustomed to. This was achieved by employing low-waged, hard-working Black porters. To be a Pullman porter meant you had a respectable job, with some prestige. You wore smart uniforms, travelled the country, met famous people, and experienced relentless racism and discrimination. Their reputation for a certain worldliness enhanced by their travel and exposure to a wide range of people gave them status and the confidence to eventually fight for their rights. Their pioneering efforts paved the way for the Black middle class.

In the way that the enslaved would take on the name of their enslaver, the porters all assumed the name "George" after George Pullman. For the porters, the inner turmoil this loss of individuality elicited had to be suppressed. They had no choice. The practice found an unlikely challenger in lumber baron George W. Dulany in 1914 when he established the Society for the Prevention of Calling Sleeping Car Porters George (SPCSCPG). Although at its peak it had 31,000 members, the society started as a cruel joke to "preserve" the dignity of those white men whose name was George rather than a cry for identity among Black porters. It did have some impact by persuading the Pullman company to put a rack in each car so that the true name of the porter on duty could be displayed.

Black porters were paid extremely low wages, relied on tips for a liveable income, and worked long hours with only a small fold-up chair to rest on when not tending to passengers. They were required to provide their own uniform, their own meals on the journey, and their own accommodations during layovers. They were responsible for greeting travellers, babysitting children, looking after sick or drunk passengers, and meeting any other need required. They also had to pay for the shoe polish used on the passengers' shoes that they would shine every night. These conditions led the porters to form a union called the Brotherhood of Sleeping Car Porters in 1925, which eventually led to better pay and working conditions and more dignity afforded to the men, a significant step on the path to racial equality, and often considered to be one of the core underpinnings of the Civil Rights Movement.

The luxury of the Pullman palace car that Sarah Bernhardt travelled in speaks to a time when having a zebra rug held cachet. Bernhardt's rug would have appealed to Lucius Beebe, an American journalist, gourmand, and train historian who travelled across the United States in Pullman cars during the first half of the twentieth century. Beebe's grandiloquent writing style can be seen in his comparison of the Pullman to a steamer on rails: "Baths, both tub and shower, barbershops, manicures, lady's maids, valet service, news tickers, libraries, current periodicals and hotel and railroad directories, smokers' accessories and, of course, the fullest possible facilities for sluicing and gentling the patrons with wines and strong waters were taken for granted on all luxury trains of the era." Beebe, along with his partner Charles Clegg, himself a train historian and photographer, would come to own two former Pullman cars—the Virginia City and The Gold Coast—that they refurbished in Victorian baroque style.

My husband, daughter, and I had our own experience of refurbished elegance when we spent a weekend in a caboose transplanted to the middle of the Ontario countryside, a modest but well-appointed renovation. With an outdoor shower and a nearby hammock, it had its charm but I came to realize that a railway car that is not moving has a different appeal. I prefer one that is in motion.

⁂

Those who could owned private cars that they would hitch to one of the named train routes in the Unites States for a fee and ride across the country in their private luxury. Marjorie Merriweather Post, the Post cereals heiress, had a train specially built in 1922 that her family used for business travel as well as for personal trips between their homes in New York City, Palm Beach, and the Adirondacks of upstate New York.

I can't help but think of the expansion of space and time that this represents, knowing that today these jaunts could be made in a few hours by private jet. From New York City to the Adirondacks must have been the better part of a day, with the train taking them as far as Lake Clear Junction, where one of their Cadillacs would be waiting to take them the two-mile journey to the yacht that would transport them across the lake to a funicular that carried them up to their retreat, Camp Topridge.

⁂

Is it not enough to travel but that some feel the need to travel in style? This is not something that weighs me down, but I think about it, the odd time I'm in a swanky hotel, assuming the air of someone who can afford such lavish living. I can enjoy the excess—of service, spotless rooms, high-thread-count sheets—because I am unfettered by the responsibility of it. There is freedom in this exchange, and a playfulness that comes with it.

This burden of excess is not evident with Lucius Beebe and Charles Clegg in the photograph I came across of them in the dining room of their private railcar, where the décor might be considered overwhelming by some. The two are sitting, wearing tuxedos, at a linen-draped table set with full service and a large bouquet of flowers. Behind Beebe at the head of the table are two decorative columns that stand at the same height as the waiter. Each column has an elaborate candelabrum on top, begging the question of how the waiter could maneuver around them carrying food and drink, not to mention the fire hazard of lit candles and swaying trains. The walls are wood panelled, and crimson drapery, tufted satiny sheers, and a valence extend the length of the car. A mirror on one end wall doubles this extravagance. The style is not to my taste, though it was very much of its time—an overdone English country manor in miniature—and it raised the bar on Pullman's original design intention of simple, increased comfort.

⁂

This shuttling around the country with candelabra at my shoulder is not something I have ever experienced. And despite the over-the-top luxury of some of these cars, it was still about that basic need to get from one place to another. I often travelled from home to university by train when I was younger, and at the time it was my own form of luxury. Hitchhiking was common then, and it was usually my preferred way of getting home—in the back of a pickup, high in the cabin of an eighteen-wheeler, in a moving truck that dropped me off a few doors from my parents' house. Hitchhiking was free and easy, and quicker. It was also safe, so we believed. A friend gave me a lift, I'd tell my parents. The bus, which I took just once, the only time I've ever had motion sickness, was a milk run. The train was the expensive option and took five hours, but that was four hours shorter than the bus. No one I knew had a car.

On those Sunday nights heading back to university when I was lucky enough to be on the train, I would pull out the stack of books I'd ambitiously dragged home. Working by the overhead light, I soon succumbed to the gentle rocking. My eyes would swerve from the page, my pen loosened from my grip, and before long my body toppled sideways, one hand reaching for my jacket to use as a pillow, sleep overtaking. Or if I was travelling with a friend, we'd go to the bar car, which was really just a cordoned-off section with a few tables and a snack counter that sold beer, the air always thick with smoke. This was an unremarkable setting, the opposite of the Pullman cars, but the atmosphere I remember well, one of lively conversation, loud voices across tables, the space so small that drinks and money and cigarettes were passed back and forth across from the counter without anyone leaving their seat.

We forget this reliance on trains to get around, now that cars and air travel have overtaken it. We have to go back to the time around World War II, when train travel was at its height, to really get a sense of its usage. Gas was rationed, cars were not plentiful, walking or horseback was an option, as was the bus, but if I were a young adult needing to get home from university or across the country to find work in the fields, or the reverse, leaving my village to go find work in the factories, it would be the train I would have taken.

As a woman, it's likely that I would be taking the train heading for one of the factory jobs vacated by men. Arriving at the station, my small suitcase in one hand, I would face a deluge of people, everyone trying to get on the trains and gain a coveted seat, the atmosphere modern commuters experience. But with the war on, everything was tinged with a sense of urgency. There would be soldiers—in England and the rest of Europe. If I were a civilian then, I would have to wait at the back of the queue, as soldiers had priority. Even for them, it could be a challenge to find a space. In the BBC WW2 People's War archives, one woman recalls her own experience of travelling around Britain: "Getting on to some trains was a nightmare. Inevitably the train would be full to the gunnels, with men on occasion hurling themselves in through the carriage's open windows, and if the seats were already full, they would climb on to the luggage rack."

If I were lucky enough to go on holiday then, I would have to take the train, perhaps so full I might be forced to stand for the entire journey. If I went to the toilet, I might come across people playing cards in the washroom. There would be a party atmosphere to it all, not unlike the crowded bar car in my own university days, the sense that we're all in it together, whatever "it" was.

That period when the ordinary became the extraordinary no longer exists on trains. The atmosphere of merriment, or the extravagance of Pullman cars is lost, except for the elite who can afford to create their own version of it. What if it returned, I want to know.

But there is a train renaissance underway. We are looking at train travel in a new light, whether through a sense of environmental responsibility or a desire for a slower form of travel. We are becoming more reliant on them again, and are growing used to this being a valid and desired travel option, whether it's a business trip to the capital or a voyage on the Rocky Mountaineer.

The *Oxford Dictionary* defines renaissance as "any revival, or period of marked improvement and new life, in art, literature, etc.," and in thinking about train travel, it is the Pullman fantasy that I think of, rather than the sleek, high speed, ergonomic overnight trains that are being developed. I am seeking glamour as well as efficiency, so in thinking of the renaissance, I am harking back to the self-contained world like the one Bernhardt commanded for her tour. It seems like the right kind of dreamspace to occupy.

There was much speculation that after this time of global isolation we would enter a period of hedonism and high-living, but it's not this I wanted so much as inspired train travel, the kind that would elevate its status once again. Even as things returned to normal, I imagined being on such a train—my

own Pullman palace—one that would take me far from where
I was.

⁂

For Bernhardt, stranded on that Christmas morning, there was
nothing to do but wait out the storm, so the cooks prepared
Christmas dinner with what they had, and they settled down
for the night. In the morning the Urania Hill cut had been
nearly filled with snow so that the train was completely covered except for the chimney holes. The engineer dug his way
out and walked to a nearby farm, returning with fresh bread,
eggs, butter, and sausage for a country breakfast. The rescue
train arrived later that morning carrying a hundred men with
shovels to dig them out. By three in the afternoon, they were
on their way, in time for the evening performance. Bernhardt
gave each of the crew a pass to the show.

Borders

A great traveller (in distinction to a merely good one) is a kind of introspective; as she covers the ground outwardly, so she advances towards fresh interpretations of herself inwardly.

—Lawrence Durrell, foreword to
The Journey's Echo: Selections from Freya Stark

Just beyond our backyard, at a drop of some twenty feet, lies a railtrack that slices through our city. After several months of thinking and writing of trains, I am aware of the track's proximity anew, and its constancy in the background of my life. Trains are with me even when I'm not travelling. When our daughter was young, each night at around six p.m. she would stop what she was doing and hurl herself towards the back fence, shouting "the train" and stand watching the top of it pass by. Sometimes the engineer would see her and wave.

The six p.m. train no longer goes through, but sometimes one passes around ten p.m., and later still, there is another around three a.m. that I hear if I can't sleep. I will feel the soft rumblings of the locomotive approaching, and if I'm groggy I will be confused, thinking a thunderstorm is brewing.

We have become so accustomed to trains occupying our urban space that this track is barely noticed, and once out into the countryside the rails blend into the landscape, invisible unless a train happens to travel along them. When we lived in Illinois, even though our apartment was in the centre of the twin cities of Champaign-Urbana, I would hear the long, lonesome wail of a country-crossing train whistle every night. It never felt like an intrusion, perhaps because of my love for trains, but also because they are so entwined with our ideas of movement and progress that it's easy to forget that they have been with us for just two centuries.

In Europe, the development of railways can be traced to the rise of steam power and to the impact of war. The French Revolution and the Napoleonic Wars, during which so many horses were killed, made it clear a new system of transportation was needed. Great Britain pioneered train travel with the first public railway to use steam locomotives, the Stockton and Darlington, opened in 1825. Other European countries developed their own railways soon after in a spurt of growth so great that thousands of miles of track were laid within each country. By 1900, the tracks crossed borders and all of Europe became connected by rail.

Because it is fairly straightforward to travel from one country to the next in Europe, it is easy to forget how the railway played a part in moving goods and people across boundaries to new cultures so that they became less remote and people more aware of the differences and similarities between them. Communities were no longer as isolated when Europe became connected by a grid of railways. And with that opening up came a weakening of identity as people no longer had to travel to another locality to purchase their distinct goods. You no longer had to cross the border to get cheese from France, the cheese would come to you. The world opened up and new products and ideas flowed across national borders, but perhaps some things have been lost in that new homogeneity.

＊

Not long after the fall of Communism, when I was living in Poland, I decided to take a weekend journey to Prague. I was on the train, in a compartment with five strangers. In this enclosed room, I sat still, reading my book, looking out the window, aware that conversation was not possible, language a barrier that prevented anything other than rudimentary exchanges.

The sound of footfalls in the corridor roused us all, heavy boots thumping, the sounds of doors opening, closing, then they were at our door, three men in uniform. Those loud thudding steps ring clear as they play back to me like a scene in a movie— the moment of waiting, the sense of something ominous about to happen. When they appeared, they looked to me to be soldiers but they were actually border control. We all sat up straighter, watched them slide open the door, until a voice called out, loud and barking, Documents!

I had come to know trepidation in the face of authority during my time in Poland—once when I was caught jay-walking, two policemen stopped me and my work colleague and immediately asked for our documents. My colleague, who was Polish-Canadian and more fluent than me, was able to talk our way out of it, but it was a lesson to me in the power of authority, when the possibility that the simple act of walking across a street might land you in trouble. When you cross borders, all the rules change.

On that train to Prague we handed over our documents, silent all, and the soldiers moved on. Their briskness was a leftover from the time when the whims of those in command were to be feared, and this fear the basis of their control. We went back to our books, our newspapers, our staring out the window. It was a strange way to enter a country.

My daughter has three nationalities: American by birth; British from her father; and Canadian from me. We use the passport of the country we're entering when travelling with her, aware that her options of where to work and live give her privileges few have. It was a South African friend who first introduced the idea of passport as a privilege, by the urgency with which she sought her Canadian passport when she moved here. She explained that it gave her the freedom to cross borders without question. I was unused to this idea of being challenged at the border—my childhood road trip crossings into the United States with my parents were done with a faint wave of their driving licence, no photo identification required, while we played in the backseat.

Now crossing borders with a passport is commonplace and a time when passports weren't needed seems unthinkable, though it was only during World War I that Europe introduced passports as a security measure to keep track of emigration and those with useful skills.

In writing about the period before passports were required, Stefan Zweig revealed that he had "travelled from Europe to India and to America without passport and without ever having seen one. One embarked and alighted without questioning or being questioned, one did not have to fill out a single one of the many papers which are required today."

This changed dramatically during the war so that, as he describes it somewhat facetiously, there "had to be photographs from right and left, in profile and full face, one's hair had to be cropped sufficiently to make the ears visible; fingerprints were taken, at first only the thumb but later all ten fingers; furthermore, certificates of health, of vaccination, police certificates of good standing, had to be shown; letters of recommendation were required, invitations to visit a country had to be produced; they asked for the addresses of relatives, for moral and financial guarantees, questionnaires, and forms in triplicate and quadruplicate needed to be filled out, and if only one of this sheaf of papers was missing one was lost."

It would be a little while longer before I'd need my passport again, but still I looked ahead to future trips. As Covid waned, we could again board trains, planes, and see loved ones after so much time. Despite the complications of travel and new variants, people are travelling again.

I booked my first train in over two years, the 5:39 a.m. commuter from Kitchener, changing in Toronto, bound for Montreal. I slept well the night before despite the concern about a failed alarm, or missing my train, or the excitement of travelling again. I walked to the station through steady rain, the soft patter on my umbrella somehow cheering me. The streets slick with the early morning downpour and the quiet of the neighbourhood so noticeable that the steady thrum of my wheeled suitcase seemed amplified. I arrived at the station ten minutes early, damp, and slightly worried that I'd got it all wrong. There was no train, no other passengers. Soon, though, a taxi pulled up and a man obviously unaccustomed to early morning chatter studiously avoided me. The rain continued. Still no train.

Then a beam down the line, a beacon for the few who had gathered because now it was the 6:03 a.m. train we were waiting for and more passengers had arrived. I boarded the train, losing my confidence in my ability to make the connecting train. But no, the 6:03 was on time as it rolled into Toronto. Then, at the moment we arrived into the station I received an email informing me that my next train had been cancelled.

This abrupt change of plan meant a rush to the information desk, then a swift abandoning of the queue to run back to the outgoing commuter trains, where I would board the last one to leave that morning to take me back home. Upon arriving back in Kitchener I would take the car, now filled with gas and a sizable packed lunch sitting on the passenger seat, and drive the six and a half hours to Montreal.

So, this is what it's like to travel again, I thought as rain lashed the car. I looked back at myself in the chaos of the morning, frustrated yes, but also full of the energy needed to navigate a plan that had strayed way off course. In the dullness of spending so much time at home over the past years, I'd come to wonder what I was still capable of as a traveller. And in writing about the journeys I'd made over the years, I was struck by a constant reaching out I'd demonstrated at the time, a kind of searching that defined my travels, and a reminder of the risk-taking I'd taken when travelling alone.

Rebecca Solnit, writing in *Recollections of My Nonexistence* about living in San Francisco in her youth, said, "It was an era of both more unpredictable contact and more profound solitude." This is a fitting description of my own experience in my early travels. In revisiting some of those journeys I've been able to see that I had a need for some sort of connection, that I was looking for meaning in the places I visited, often with a sense of urgency. But I was also often alone.

Over the past two decades the story of my travel has changed. Travel taken alone has given way to those taken with my husband and child. Each has its own accumulated memories. I am out in the world in a different way, less exposed and searching than I was in those early years, now with a kind of ease, a quiet contentment that allows me to read or nap or play games, or to sit and look at others on the train or outside my window. I am still somewhere far from home, still reaching out in some way and yet, perhaps oddly, it is the fact of being away that allows me to be restful, to be fully there.

I crossed many borders in lockdown, though they were all done from my study. I mined memories and recreated new versions of trips so that I now wonder what the real journey was—the physical one taken at the time or the internal one I've taken in writing about it. I am following the tradition of other women writers who have approached their travel memoir as a way of exploring their own evolving thoughts and impressions.

What does travel literature do but recreate something with our own slant, from memory and emotions, selecting the elements that mean something? In her introduction to *The Virago Book of Women Travellers*, Mary Morris talks about the lack of travel literature by women and the differences between that written by men and women. She writes that for men, for the most part, it is the external that is essential; these male writers reveal only glimpses of themselves, who they miss in being there, what impression the place has on them. The writer's inner workings are largely obscured. "For women, the inner landscape is as important as the outer, the beholder as important as the beheld. The landscape is shaped by the consciousness of the person who crosses it. There is a dialogue between what is happening within and without."

This dialogue between the inner and outer has surprised me, as if I thought I could just sit down and re-tell the story by documenting the sights. But it was not enough to remember the physical features of those places I'd visited, I realized. I had to immerse myself, to revisit the person I was at the time, because that was part of the story. In navigating this inner and outer journey I discovered that in some ways, the journey never really ended, it lives inside me and this became my comfort when I was restricted from going anywhere.

In Elizabeth Bishop's poem "Questions of Travel" the narrator has her own wavering doubts and convictions about the merits of travelling. "Think of the long trip home," she writes. "Should we have stayed at home and thought of here?"

The question of whether to go or stay is never really a question for me. Even in those periods when we were not permitted to leave our home, I was away somewhere.

Later in the poem, Bishop writes:

Oh, must we dream our dreams
and have them, too?
And have we room
for one more folded sunset, still quite warm?

The answer, of course, is yes.

Afterword

It's true that when the end already seems near,
there is always still a stretch of time left.

—Lalla Romano, *A Silence Shared*

We were all waiting for the revelry to begin. We were told, in the way of an urban legend, with no discernable source, that once this was all over it would be like the Roaring Twenties. I wanted glittery shift dresses, shots of whiskey, the rousing notes of big band jazz as a constant soundtrack. And, of course, to travel again.

We knew not when the end of the plague would come. Pandemics dwindle down, they make for a messy, chaotic conclusion, or so I'd read early on. That meant travel started up in an equally messy way. Where was the joy that was our earned right? Instead, we were stumbling out of mandates, looking for a finish line that was not so easily drawn. People talked of freedom. Some tired of the restrictions and used the rhetoric of enslavement. By the eighth wave, anger and frustration were in good supply, and returning to normal seemed elusive, just out of our reach. We all just wanted to bring the party inside.

It was in the midst of this disquiet that I booked the annual train journey with my daughter to the Maritimes. A few months later we set off, but things had changed. The passenger train that we'd taken on the first leg had now been cancelled, so we were left with a commuter train. We hauled our luggage on the double-decker train and looked for a place where we would be less conspicuous, where we could hide the fact that we were travellers not workers. There were no racks for luggage storage so we found ourselves jammed into seats by the door, facing a wall, our bags stacked around us. Clearly, a reset was needed. We had to remember how to travel again.

We eventually found a window seat but our chattel remained teetering statues at our feet. We changed trains in Toronto and were masked for much of the trip until we reached Montreal, when we found refuge in our cabin. The dining car, once something we looked forward to on our trip as a chance to meet others over a meal, was eerily quiet, and we soon realized that the train was running at reduced capacity. It was so sparsely populated that no one sat with us at any of the sittings.

Ensconced in our cabin, the notion of retreat that I'd come to identify with the train had taken on a new layer of self-preservation. Still, we were back on the train, not only physically but we were also slowly entering the mindset we'd had in the past, so that it felt like an off-kilter homecoming in a similar vein experienced by Stefan Zweig, who considered the train not a departure from home but a home itself. He invariably packed two suitcases, one with clothes, the other with manuscripts he was working on. "Whatever it might be, to travel is for me no longer something foreign, but almost natural. One breaks free with more force from one's ties and habits, of one's home and possessions . . ."

❧

Months later, still looking for the Roaring Twenties vibe, still aware of the tentativeness that lingered with travel and the low-level tension that we'd felt on that first journey back, I was in need of a kind of lightness. We'd been cautious for so long, even as we started to return to what we'd relentlessly dubbed "normal" living, the uncertainty was like a constant background hum to all our lives. When this lightness came, it appeared in the form of a young trainspotter. On TikTok, no less.

Trainspotting, I remembered as a particularly British pastime practised by individuals who stand on train platforms collecting the numbers from incoming locomotives and record them in a notebook. They are mostly men, and mostly mocked as "anoraks," or one who has an obsessive interest in a subject.

Although the golden age of trainspotting took place during the 1950s, its origins go back to 1861 with the first trainspotter said to be a young woman, fourteen-year-old Londoner Fanny Johnson, whose notebook recording train numbers to and from Paddington was reproduced in the *Great Western Railway Magazine* in 1935. Trainspotting gained traction in the UK in the 1940s when a young railway worker, Ian Allan, working at Waterloo Station, thought a guide might be useful for young train enthusiasts who often wrote to the train company asking for information about the trains. The rail company didn't agree to making a guide so he took it on himself and also formed a "loco-spotting" club.

I'd remembered reading an article in *The Guardian* about Francis Bourgeois, a trainspotter who had a following on TikTok that was nearing five million. I'd read about his animated videos in appreciation of railways, his wild exhilaration with each spotting that often had him in a fit of giggles, and more recently his taste for vintage clothes—or designer now that Gucci has come on board—so that he appears to have just walked off an Agatha Christie movie set. Here was a man in his early twenties, gleefully filming the trains and his reactions to their arrival with a GoPro attached to his head. It was rapture incarnate.

But what was it that made him so happy—the train itself? The act of spotting of the train? Where was the pleasure in all this? To be a trainspotter is to practice a particular way of seeing, it is the hunt of the collector—of laying claim to something esoteric that has value others may not recognize. Here, the train is an object to be collected, just as some choose stamps or coins for the same purpose, and there is an urge to classify that offers a sense of order not often found in our lives.

How different this is from my perspective. I'm not seeking order when I enter the train, in fact it may be a form of disorder or disruption that I want when I'm travelling, of releasing myself from the habits and stale thoughts that come with routine, to allow myself to be an observer from the inside looking at the fleeting landscape, the perfect platform for my mind to drift and soar. For me it is not so much seeing the train as seeing from it.

To watch Francis Bourgeois as he whooped and wowed his way through the videos was just a reminder of how careful we'd been, how guarded. Had we lost the art of jubilation? The past few years has made observers of us, but not in the way of a traveller. Sometimes our seeing has been laden: we have been wary, watchful of the behaviour of others, sometimes judgmental. Bourgeois said trains stimulate him in inexplicable ways: "Possibly it's hard to comprehend how good I feel about trains; how good I can feel full stop." I have further understanding of his state of mind when he talks about the unique language that goes with it—livery is the paint job; thrash is the sound that diesel engines make when they open up; clag is the exhaust. And "hellfire" is an expression of real joy and elation.

Hellfire, indeed! Could this be the emissary to announce that glory days had indeed returned? That the Roaring Twenties might be arriving after all?

Now, a few months after the pandemic has been declared officially over by the World Health Organization, with continued warnings to maintain caution as Covid is still brewing, I am back on the train again. Literally as I write this but also I am back on the train metaphorically, having entered the psychic space where there is some freedom to travel, the window gazing from my study no longer an endless pastime. I can inhabit the possibilities in this world again. I've been thinking about how to end this meditation on travel, this revisiting of all those train journeys that saw me through the pandemic and, of course, it has to end where it began, on the train.

Thinking back on our return journey on the Ocean, where the cabin again offered the quiet isolation we needed, it was as though we were being tested. We awoke to find that we were running two hours late, which meant missing our connection in Montreal. It was VIA Rail's responsibility to get us home, so this was not so much a worry, but something to keep an eye on, something that kept us checking the time and arrival updates. It fed into that nervous watchfulness we'd cultivated the past few years. We did indeed miss the train, but were upgraded to business class on the next leg, which allowed us the privilege of space as, even fully masked, we were always measuring the distance, thinking of how far Covid particles could travel. This train, too, was late, causing us to miss the only connection to Kitchener. With no other options, we were sent home in a taxi, windows open, masks on. Three days later, my husband tested positive for Covid, the next day I did, the following day our daughter, too, was stricken.

I put my pencil down to stare out the window for a while, and soon we pass four freight cars, lying on the side of the tracks like a child's toys tossed aside. These are the remnants of a derailment four months ago, which seems like an apt representation of these times. It is strange to see them there, banged up and rusting, discarded beside the embankment. It is as though they are a manifestation and a reminder of what we've been through all at once. One day they will be relics disconnected from the pandemic, but for now they seem so very much of this time.

Will I think of train travel as a right or a privilege from now on? We thought that this "great pause" would change us, make us appreciate what we took for granted. We took on slow living and thought it would remain this way, we'd been rushing around for too long. We would stay home more, venture out to nearby campsites, cottages, or tourist sites when this is done. We would be changed.

However, the signs are that this was not to be. As soon as travel restrictions lifted, the floodgate opened and the airports were filled. This should not be a surprise. We have been conditioned to travel to the other side of the world in a matter of hours. We cannot reverse time; we cannot erase the experience of travel. But the shock of losing all those trips has altered the way I view travel. There is uncertainty that didn't exist before, with cancelled flights or train journeys more a possibility than before; we know how easy it can be taken from us. Could the idea of travel as a disruptor in our lives take on new meaning here? I've seen travel as an escape from routine, a disruption that colours my life rather than thwarts its rituals. These last few years has shown me that it's a privilege, despite, or because of the uncertainty. Will I chance it? Always.

This train journey, taken to Montreal to see my daughter, feels like a truer return. The train is half empty, the sun is shining, and like Stefan Zweig, I have one bag of clothes, another with books and notebooks. I write for a while, then read, sometimes lifting my eyes to the streaming vista outside my window. There is Lake Ontario, there is the nuclear plant, there is Cobourg, which I really should visit one day. I'm thinking about the end of this book, and what it's given me to write it during this time of isolation, and I'm thinking ahead to the research I have to do on my next book because I need to have something to pull me forward. My mind feels expansive in this enclosed space—it drifts and winnows into thought crevices so that I feel my inner life flourishing while my outer life, in its fleeting nature, stabilizes me. I am at last still while moving forward at the same time.

Selected
Bibliography

Bradley, Simon. *The Railways: Nation, Network & People*.
London: Profile Books, 2016.

Daschuk, James. *Clearing the Plains: Disease, Politics of
Starvation, and the Loss of Indigenous Life*. Regina:
University of Regina Press, 2019.

Defoe, Daniel. *A Journal of the Plague Year*. The Project
Gutenberg ebook, 1995, 2023.

Diski, Jenny. *Stranger on a Train: Daydreaming and Smoking
around America with Interruptions*. London: Virago, 2002,
2004.

Colquhoun, Kate. *Mr Briggs' Hat: A Sensational Account of
Britain's First Railway Murder*. London: Harry N. Abrams,
2011.

Garrett, Evan. "Sarah Bernhardt's Christmas in Urania." *Ann
Arbor Observer*.

Goldsmith, Barbara. *Other Powers: The Age of Suffrage,
Spiritualism, and the Scandalous Victoria Woodhull*. New
York: Harper Perennial, 1999.

Goodman, Edward C., ed. *Writing the Rails: Train Adventures by the World's Best-Loved Writers*. New York: Black Dog & Leventhal, 2001.

Leigh Fermor, Patrick. *A Time of Gifts*. London: John Murray, 1977, 2013.

Levy, Deborah. *Real Estate*. London: Hamish Hamilton, 2021.

Mead, Margaret. *A Way of Seeing*. United States: McCall Publishing Company, 1970.

Morris, Jan. *Trieste and the Meaning of Nowhere*. Faber & Faber, 2002.

Morris, Mary, with Larry O'Connor, eds. *The Virago Book of Women Travellers*. Great Britain: Virago, 1994, 2020.

Schivelbusch, Wolfgang. *The Railway Journey: The Industrialization of Time and Space in the Nineteenth Century*. Berkley, California: University of California Press, 1977, 1986.

Shelley, Mary. *History of a Six Weeks' Tour Through a Part of France, Switzerland, Germany, and Holland*. London: T. Hookham, 1817.

Smith, Douglas N.W. *The Ocean Limited: A Centennial Tribute*. Ottawa: Douglas N.W. Smith, 2004.

Whitman, James Q. *Hitler's American Model: The United States and the Making of the Nazi Race Law*. Princeton, N.J.: Princeton University Press, 2017.

Wollstonecraft, Mary. *Letters Written During a Short Residence in Sweden, Norway and Denmark*. Wilmington, Delaware: J. Wilson, 1796.

Zweig, Stefan. *Journeys*. London: Pushkin Press, 2019.

Acknowledgements

This book would not have moved beyond a scrambled idea to an actual manuscript without the mentorship of Helen Humphreys—her boundless wisdom, support, and genius when it comes to the craft of writing has long inspired me. Susan Renouf's enthusiasm for a book about train travel was immediate, and I am eternally grateful for her guidance in getting the manuscript into shape. Thanks also to Jen Knoch for her astute and careful copy editing. I am grateful, too, to Jessica Albert for overseeing the splendid design of the book, and to Caroline Suzuki for her creative eye on the gorgeous book cover. A huge thanks to Claire Pokorchak for taking care of the marketing and publicity. Thanks also to Victoria Cozza and everyone else at ECW Press who had a hand in getting this book out into the world.

Off the Tracks has been a long time in the making and over the years I've shared ideas and extracts with people who have supported me throughout, including Caroline Ball, Erin Bow, Marsha Cameron, Sheila Cameron, Stacey Cameron, Susan Fish, Nan Forler, Julie Friesen, Kim Knowles, Pegi MacKay,

Yashin Masoliver, Kristen Mathies, Margie Matlack, Ann Mulloy, Susan Scott, and Anna Trinca.

For his assistance on the subject of spiritualism, I'd like to thank Nick Richbell.

The seed of this book came twenty years ago, when I was living in Illinois and a friend recommended Wolfgang Schivelbusch's *The Railway Journey: The Industrialization of Time and Space in the Nineteenth Century* when I said I was considering writing a book about trains. At the time I didn't know whether it would be fiction or nonfiction, but I devoured Schivelbusch's book. It helped shaped my way of thinking about trains and became a considerable influence on my writing about the subject.

The Railways: Nation, Network & People by Simon Bradley also provided a rich and comprehensive history of railway travel. The detailed facts and anecdotes helped enhance my own book, and for anyone who has an interest in trains, it's a fascinating read.

The research I undertook was wide and varied and I've provided a selected bibliography of key sources. Numerous online archives, newsletters, newspaper articles, and books provided inspiration in the multiple directions my meditations took during the writing process. The rabbit hole of research often proved to be a fruitful use of time.

I am deeply grateful to Rose Hendrie for her editorial hand and Kyle Wyatt for publishing an excerpt of the book in the *Literary Review of Canada*.

I would like to thank the Canada Council for the Arts for the financial support they provided in the writing of the book.

Thanks, finally, to Darren, my life partner, my constant everything, and to Esme, who continues to inspire me in so many ways. My finest, abiding travel companions.